The FRIENDSHIP BOOK

of Francis Gay

D.C. THOMSON & CO., LTD.
London Glasgow Manchester Dundee

A Thought
For Each Day
In 2002

May the hinges of friendship never rust,
nor the wings of love lose a feather.
                    Old Toast.

OLD RUGGED CROSS

January

AT the beginning of this new year I wish, in the words of the poet Samuel Coleridge, that "all seasons shall be sweet to you", and that you will know the warmth of friendship as you travel through the coming months.

OUR friend Mary passed this little verse on to me and I think you'll enjoy reading it. She saw it in her doctor's waiting-room and it made an immediate impression. The sentiments are worth keeping in mind at any time:

Smiling is Infectious,
You catch it like the flu.
When someone smiled at me today
I started smiling, too.

I passed around the corner,
And someone saw my grin,
When he smiled, I realised
I'd passed it on to him.

If you feel a smile begin
Don't leave it undetected,
Let's start an epidemic
And get the world infected!

THURSDAY—JANUARY 3.

ON the outside of the New Year card which the Lady of the House and I received one year was a photograph of the hushed splendour of a country garden under snow. Inside our friends had written:

"We wish you both in the coming year an increase in faith, love and may you always see a patch of blue when skies are grey, and find a sprinkle of stars to add a sparkle to your life."

A lovely message of good wishes which the Lady of the House and I would like to pass on to you as you open the pages of "The Friendship Book" at the start of another year.

FRIDAY—JANUARY 4.

OUR friend Mhairi arrived home from an amateur writers' meeting one evening looking pleased with herself. "I was given a new title," she told her husband and went on to explain.

She and her friends had each taken a poem or piece of prose to read aloud. She had read one of her own compositions, and it was well received.

"One friend described me as a 'wordsmith'. Now, wasn't that nice?" she remarked.

Her husband agreed that it was and it is a delightful word to use. We all know how silversmiths, goldsmiths and blacksmiths create wonderful things. Sometimes, the rest of us only have words to offer each other. If we choose them carefully, we can also create something of value.

SATURDAY—JANUARY 5.

WHEN I dismantle our Christmas tree after all the festivities, the decorations and tinsel are put back into their box and I take down our angel from the top. It is very special to us — it is made of straw and came from Africa.

As I admire our straw angel I think of all the angels in our community. They often seem very ordinary and unassuming, too. They work in our hospitals, hospices, children's homes and also care for the elderly and younger disadvantaged folk. They are all those whose kindness, patience and friendship for others is unstinting.

When I put away our plain, yet beautiful angel, I always think of those who may be taken for granted — the angels amongst us who work so hard for others.

SUNDAY—JANUARY 6.

HOLD fast the form of sound words, which thou hast heard of me, in faith and love which is in Christ Jesus.

Timothy II 1:13

MONDAY—JANUARY 7.

"THOUGH the harvest you may not see, each kindly act is an acorn dropped in God's productive soil."

Just a few words, but they say a great deal, and give much food for thought, too. They were wtitten by the popular American writer Ella Wheeler Wilcox, born in 1856.

MAKING
TRACKS

TUESDAY—JANUARY 8.

IT is cold, so cold. The frost has the earth in its grasp, and the trees stand stiff in their coats of rime. We shiver, and think, will Winter never end?

Take heart, for the earth is just sleeping and renewing its strength. Soon it will awaken, the green shoots will start to appear, and the sun will gradually gain strength and warmth. Just like life, in fact.

From time to time we all need a period of rest in which to think and restore our jaded spirits, a peaceful interlude to reflect, to plan, and give ourselves strength for the days ahead. Keep that thought in mind, and today's cold and frost will surely be full of hope for the future.

WEDNESDAY—JANUARY 9.

THOMAS The Tank Engine is much loved by generations of youngsters, originally created by the Rev. Wilbert Awdry. He was a Church of England rector who invented characters which embody, in part, his philosophy of life: "This world is God's world. We have free choice. We can obey or disobey. If we disobey, we bring trouble on ourselves and on other people."

His engines have human foibles — they often go their own way and then learn valuable lessons about life. Those who appreciate Thomas The Tank Engine and his friends would gladly echo Rev. Awdry's epitaph: "He helped people to see God in the ordinary things of life, and he made children laugh."

THURSDAY—JANUARY 10.

I ONCE heard this story about John Wesley. It seems he was walking along a country lane with a friend who had many problems. The man said he couldn't see the way ahead, or even think which way to turn.

Wesley paused and drew his friend's attention to the thick hedge beside them. It was impossible to see through it and yet they were able to look over it. This was the only solution in a difficult situation, he explained.

If we can see a distant horizon or a glimpse of blue sky, it's easier to deal with our troubles. So, when you can't see through the hedge surrounding you, look over it!

FRIDAY—JANUARY 11.

MARK'S job is to help with the rehabilitation of ex-prisoners. It takes a dedicated man to tackle such a job, and Mark is certainly that. As a result of his concern and practical help many men and women now live responsible lives, supporting their families, and respected in the community.

I got to know one of the young men he had set on the right road, and he was enthusiastic about just what Mark had done for him. "I've never forgotten one most important thing he told me," he said. "It was this — 'No matter what wrong you did to spoil your past, just remember you have a spotless future ahead'."

What a positive attitude to pass on . . . to anyone.

**FLYING
COLOURS**

SATURDAY—JANUARY 12.

AS part of her college course Tessa had to undertake a photography project. She chose the architecture of old buildings. When she had finished, she went round to show the results to a neighbour.

"Why, they're fascinating!" enthused Avril. "I love all these small details that you've captured. You must have travelled about quite a bit to find material for all these shots."

Tessa laughed. "I didn't go anywhere," she said, "except around our own town here. But it's amazing how easy it is to find things of interest when you actually start looking."

It's good to see that Tessa's project has taught her about more than just photography!

SUNDAY—JANUARY 13.

BUT the Lord of hosts shall be exalted in judgement, and God that is holy shall be sanctified in righteousness. Isaiah 5:16

MONDAY—JANUARY 14.

ONE day I overheard someone say in a bus queue: "Oh, I can't be bothered with that — it's just a waste of time."

I don't know just what the young woman was talking about, but her words reminded me of something which Benjamin Franklin said in one of his speeches: "Do not waste time, for that is the stuff life is made of."

TUESDAY—JANUARY 15.

THANK You Lord, for the special times,
Those days I set apart,
The times of joy and happiness
Are stored within my heart.
Thank You for the days of youth
When all the world was new,
When plans and schemes were only dreams
That never would come true.

Thank You for those other times
When things went sadly wrong,
Through love and care and answered prayer,
You helped me to be strong.
For all the happy special times,
So many I recall,
For joy and tears, throughout the years,
Lord, thank You, for them all.
                                        Iris Hesselden.

WEDNESDAY—JANUARY 16.

THE town centre was busy, despite the rain. People scurried here and there, splashing through puddles with dripping umbrellas.

Leaving a shop, I paused behind a young man and his small daughter. He fastened her coat and tied her hood, before they stepped out. She looked up and said, "Oh, Dad, you're extra special!"

He and I looked at each other and I told him, "Treasure that."

He laughed and said she probably just wanted something new, but he was obviously touched. Suddenly, the afternoon didn't seem as gloomy . . .

THURSDAY—JANUARY 17.

WE were sitting relaxing quietly after supper one evening with our friends Bob and Pat when the Lady of the House suddenly asked what they would do if they had their lives to live over again.

"I would perhaps have talked less and listened more," Bob mused.

"I would have invited more friends in for a cup of tea and a chat, and worried less about the stains on the carpet and the fading fabric on the sofa," said Pat with a smile.

Soon we had a good-going discussion under way. We eventually decided that there should be time for many more moments when we should use the words, "I love you" and "I'm sorry".

FRIDAY—JANUARY 18.

THE author shook his head. He was not satisfied with the novel he was writing and pushed his manuscript into a drawer.

Nine years went by then, one day, he came across his neglected work. He re-read it and decided that it might be worth working on again. When completed, he did not have it published under his own name. If it was a failure it might discredit his poetry, or so he imagined.

"Waverley" became a resounding success — the first of Sir Walter Scott's popular historical romances. Sometimes we may believe that all our efforts seem to be in vain but we should never underestimate what we can achieve.

SATURDAY—JANUARY 19.

IN the kitchen of a bright and cosy little cottage at the foot of a hillside in the Scottish Highlands I came across this framed inscription:

"Memories are everyone's second chance at happiness."

The words took on an extra significance when I looked more closely and saw the name of the person who had spoken them — a much respected lady whose recollections in a long and event-filled life surely gave her, when she said this, the right to savour happy memories by the thousand — Elizabeth, The Queen Mother.

SUNDAY—JANUARY 20.

REMEMBER not the sins of my youth, nor my transgressions: according to thy mercy remember thou me for thy goodness' sake, O Lord.

Psalms 25:7

MONDAY—JANUARY 21.

HERE are some thought-provoking words from George Washington Carver (1864-1943), the eminent American scientist and thinker:

"How far you go in life depends on your being tender with the young, compassionate with the aged, sympathetic with the striving, and tolerant of the weak and the strong. Because, some day in your own life, you will have been all of these people yourself."

PROMISE OF
SPRING

TUESDAY—JANUARY 22.

MY thought for today comes from the pen of the Victorian clergyman and writer Charles Kingsley:

No cloud across the sun
But passes at last,
And gives us back
The face of God once more.

Those are hopeful, comforting and uplifting words to cheer us on our way on dark days in our lives.

WEDNESDAY—JANUARY 23.

OUR friend Jim has been in charge of tending the churchyard for more than half his lifetime now, and it always looks neat and attractive. But, like many of us, Jim doesn't like to admit that passing years can take their toll, so he wasn't particularly welcoming when, last year, assistance arrived in the form of Darren, a young volunteer.

At first, as Jim readily acknowledged, things were difficult. "But then," he told me, "I realised something that made me see things differently. You see, I suddenly saw that Darren needed my skills just as much as I needed his. He had the energy — but I had the skill and experience. And as soon as I realised that, I stopped feeling sorry for myself, and now we work really well together."

Looking round at the tidy churchyard, more attractive than ever, I couldn't help thinking that there's a lot to be said for teamwork.

THURSDAY—JANUARY 24.

A NEIGHBOUR of ours, Christine, was in Tokyo for a holiday one Summer and she brought home a little book of Japanese proverbs. The one which she singled out and passed on was: "One kind word can warm three Winter months".

It can help more people than you think when you say a kind word or two and take away the bitter chill.

FRIDAY—JANUARY 25.

WHEN Robert Burns was dying his wife engaged a young girl, Jessie Lewars, to help care for him. A pretty, cheerful lass, Jessie proved a real tonic for the poet who was often in great pain, and he was also racked with worries as to what would happen to his wife and children after he died.

So grateful was he that the last song he ever wrote he dedicated to Jessie. To the end of her long life Jessie treasured these lovely words:

O, wert thou in the cauld blast,
On yonder lea, on yonder lea,
*My plaidie to the angry airt,**
I'd shelter thee, I'd shelter thee.
Or did misfortune's bitter storms
Around thee blaw, around thee blaw,
Thy bield+ should be my bosom,
To share it a', to share it a'.

* direction (of the wind)
+ shelter

SATURDAY—JANUARY 26.

RIGHT in the heart of New York, a friend of ours came across these thought-provoking words on a church notice-board:

What Is Charity?
It is Silence — when your words would hurt.
It is Patience — when your neighbour is curt.
It is Deafness — when a scandal flows.
It is Thoughtfulness — for others' woes.
It is Promptness — when duty calls.
It is Courage — when misfortune falls.

SUNDAY—JANUARY 27.

IF ye abide in me, and my words abide in you, ye shall ask what ye will, and it shall be done unto you.

John 15:7

MONDAY—JANUARY 28.

ONE year my Great-Aunt Louisa spent part of January visiting friends. She later wrote in her diary:

"*28th January*. This has been a very severe Winter. There were ice crystals in the milk in the pantry this morning, and ice patterns on the inside of my bedroom window, when I recalled those fine lines by Tennyson:

Fine as ice-ferns on January panes,
Made by a breath . . .

They helped to compensate for the extreme cold and reminded me that Winter has its beauties as well as its discomforts!"

TUESDAY—JANUARY 29.

JANET was leaving home to start work for the first time, and she was extremely apprehensive. As the time grew nearer for leaving her family behind, her father, who had experienced the trauma of leaving loved ones himself, knew how she was feeling and had a chat with her.

"My mother told me one thing that I've found to be true and a comfort, as I've had to move around so much. She used to say, 'One good friend is always with you and after all, strangers are only friends that you have still to meet'!"

Janet went on her way, and made many strangers into friends.

WEDNESDAY—JANUARY 30.

I STOPPED for a minute one afternoon, to read the announcements on a country church's notice-board. One that instantly attracted my attention, stated quite simply:

"Trespassers will be forgiven!"

A neat twist, indeed, to what might at first seem a warning.

THURSDAY—JANUARY 31.

STOP a moment and dream. Dream of warm sunny Summer days; of borders and tubs full of bright blossoms; of butterflies and bees hovering over the flowers; of birds in the branches overhead singing their enjoyment of the warmth.

Yes, shut your eyes and dream . . . and remember, soon this will be reality!

February

FRIDAY—FEBRUARY 1.

OUR young friends Colin and Joanne needed to make a long journey in order to keep a hospital appointment. The appointment was early in the day and the rush-hour traffic likely to be hectic. The prospect of finding the hospital in a large city was more than a little daunting.

The evening before their visit, the Lady of the House opened a favourite book and read the following words: "For a good angel will go with him, his journey will be successful and he will come home safe and sound."

She was so inspired by these words that she phoned our friends and read the quotation to them. And yes, they did come home safe and sound. Not only that, but the medical report received later was very favourable.

May your own "Good Angel" always go with you and all those you love.

SATURDAY—FEBRUARY 2.

NOWADAYS, when both businessmen and tourists think nothing of hopping on a plane and travelling thousands of miles my thought for today seems particularly apt:

Wherever life may take you, there will always be a corner of your heart called "Home".

SUNDAY—FEBRUARY 3.

LET your heart therefore be perfect with the Lord our God, to walk in his statutes, and to keep his commandments, as at this day.

Kings I 8:61

MONDAY—FEBRUARY 4.

I'M sure you must have read at some time the famous lines of "Desiderata" which begin: "Go placidly amid the noise and haste and remember what peace there may be in silence."

Later, there is a passage which is worth recalling: "Do not distress yourself with imaginings. Many fears are born of fatigue and loneliness."

Isn't it true that we all tend to imagine things that might never happen, troubles which may never come our way? Next time you feel anxious or afraid remember these comforting lines.

TUESDAY—FEBRUARY 5.

THE first part of the prayer of St Francis Of Assisi is well known: "Where there is hatred let me sow love." Not so well known perhaps is the second verse from which I take these lines:

Grant that I may not so much seek
To be consoled as to console;
To be understood as to understand;
To be loved as to love.
For it is in giving that we receive;
It is in pardoning that we are pardoned.

MIST AND
MOUNTAIN

WEDNESDAY—FEBRUARY 6.

KEN was looking grumpy. "I've just been to a conservation group's annual general meeting," he told me one day. "You know, sometimes we don't seem to agree about anything. Have you heard the old joke that a camel is a horse designed by a committee? Well, now I know exactly what they mean!"

I laughed, and couldn't help but sympathise. Few people, however well intentioned, can be in harmony with each other all the time. And yet, if you look around, you will realise how many worthwhile projects have borne fruit from humble beginnings after folk have worked hard together to achieve a common goal.

Three cheers for committees, however annoying hold-ups can be — and I also happen to think that a camel can be a very useful animal!

THURSDAY—FEBRUARY 7.

JEREMY, who is a widower, is a good friend of ours. He comes round to see us for a chat every week, and it is usually about his young grandson James. James has changed Jeremy's life — he is a different person since James arrived.

We see endless photographs and have heard about James' first tooth and his first steps. The little walks, the chats, the swimming lessons are hours just for grandfather and grandson alone!

Being a grandparent can create a new way of life, a special bond. It is something that enriches the generations.

FRIDAY—FEBRUARY 8.

YESTERDAY will have been yet another busy twenty-four hours for many readers. Perhaps you got up early, took a hurried breakfast, went to the office or perhaps tackled household chores, maybe visited the shops, talked with friends, watched television, listened to the radio, read newspapers, washed dishes, made a few phone calls — then made plans for today.

Yet there is one task you must never forget if you share your home with a special friend, someone who waits patiently to receive a gentle word from you, a friend with an acute sense of hearing, and a rare patience to wait and wait in silence — well, almost. He or she is, of course, someone who will give you the warmest welcome of this and any day.

Just gently pat your furry four-legged friend and you'll keep the love of a faithful companion for life.

SATURDAY—FEBRUARY 9.

AN old soldier who worked with mules once told me they had taught him a great lesson.

"I realised," he said, "that when they were kickin' they weren't pullin'."

It's true. You can't do both at the same time.

SUNDAY—FEBRUARY 10.

FOR thou art my lamp, O Lord; and the Lord will lighten my darkness.
Samuel II 22:29

MONDAY—FEBRUARY 11.

I NEED no gifts of flowers,
   Your thoughts have winged their way
And framed a loving greeting
   For a very special day.

A plain and simple message
   From a dear but distant son,
The words all mothers long to hear —
   Just "Thinking of you, Mum!"

Ann Rutherford.

TUESDAY—FEBRUARY 12.

THERE are many definitions of the word "friend", but surely one of the best was given to me by Alice, who was celebrating her 100th birthday.

The guests were talking at her party about many things from the past and present, about lifestyles both old and new, and whether it is foolish to live too much in a memory-filled past. Our birthday lady, who has always believed in keeping up with the events and lifestyles of each decade she has lived through, came up with this very sound definition:

"A truly good friend," Alice said, "is the person who will always help you to put your memory years neatly behind you, but understands those very special moments when you need to hold on to them a little while longer."

Wise words for us all to keep in mind, from our centenarian.

WEDNESDAY—FEBRUARY 13.

SOME years ago Ella went to Peru with her husband who had a work placement there. He was frequently away from home, so Ella was left on her own with no friends in an unfamiliar place. She began to feel isolated and very unhappy with what had seemed at first a great adventure.

Her mother suggested that she would feel better if she tried to make friends with the folk she came into contact with and learn more about the country. Ella started to find out about the people, their language, traditions and later even wrote a book on the subject.

All this gradually changed her attitude to life abroad and what had been at first a miserable experience turned out to be a deeply rewarding one. By reaching out, she had made contact with others and brought a new dimension to her own life.

THURSDAY—FEBRUARY 14.

I'M sure that every one of us has admired the work of one of the greatest women of all time, the legendary Mother Teresa. A friend to all the world, she also possessed an insight into human behaviour and the deeds of mankind which was quite remarkable. Here is one of her memorable sayings:

"The fullness of our heart is expressed in the way we receive, in the way we need, in the way we touch, in everything that we write and say, in the way we walk, and in what others see in our eyes."

THE FRIENDSHIP BOOK

I READ this poem by John Gillespie Magee one afternoon and commend it to you today:

Oh, I have slipped the surly bonds of earth
And danced the skies on laughter-silvered wings,
Sunward I've climbed and joined the tumbling mirth
Of sun-split cloud and done a hundred things
You have not dreamed of; wheeled and soared and swung
High in the sunlit silence hov'ring there.
I've chased the shouting wind along and flung
My eager craft through footless halls of air.

Up, up the long delirious burning blue
I've topped the windswept heights with easy grace
Where never lark or even eagle flew,
And while with silent lifting mind I've trod
The high untrespassed sanctity of space
Put out my hand and touched the face of God.

"I DO like candles," remarked our young friend Lorna as she showed us her latest purchase. "They don't cost a lot," she continued, "and they create a lovely atmosphere."

There are now so many in the shops — all shapes and sizes, colours and perfumes. In this busy world, when life can be so hectic, what better way could there be to unwind than with soothing music and a little candlelight?

We all need to find our own oasis of calm and I do hope that you have discovered yours.

SUNDAY—FEBRUARY 17.

REJOICE in the Lord alway: and again I say, Rejoice.

Philippians 4:4

MONDAY—FEBRUARY 18.

F ILL every day with some kind deed
  And you'll be truly blessed,
For helping someone who's in need
  Brings peace and happiness.
And you can always guarantee
  Your day's been made worthwhile
When you take the trouble to lend a hand
  And go that extra mile.

Helena Socha.

TUESDAY—FEBRUARY 19.

ANYONE visiting Reid Park in the Scottish town of Forfar owes the experience to a poor boy and sweets. Let me explain.

Peter Reid was born on 6th October, 1803. Although his mother kept a small confectionery shop they weren't particularly well off. Peter enjoyed his schooldays, and later chose to work in his mother's shop. He started to make a special kind of rock which became popular, not merely in the Forfar area but well beyond.

Reid's Rock made Peter wealthy, and he decided to use his money to benefit his fellow citizens. His memorial is not only a lovely park called after him, but also a hospital wing and a fine public hall. Truly, he shared what he had been given so that all could benefit.

WEDNESDAY—FEBRUARY 20.

HAVE you ever thought just how many beautiful things in the world are blue?

They come in many shades — for example, stately blue delphiniums, blue skies and Summer seas, distant blue mountains, cornflowers and bluebells, the rich blues of stained glass, the blues of sapphires, aquamarines, and blue topazes . . . They all lift the heart and remind me of these lines by the Victorian writer John Ruskin:

"Blue colour is everlastingly appointed by the Deity to be a source of delight."

THURSDAY—FEBRUARY 21.

THE Lady of the House and I were out doing some shopping when we bumped into Jenny and her little boy. Young Sam was looking rather sorry for himself.

"I've got a cold," he snuffled in response to our enquiries. "And it's much worse than anyone else's, because it's *me* who's got it!"

It was impossible not to laugh, but Sam's remark did set me thinking. Nobody can blame a five-year-old for being a little self-centred, but I do wonder how many of us carry this attitude into adulthood. How many of us brood that our troubles are far worse than those suffered by others, merely because they are happening to *us*?

So next time you start feeling particularly sorry for yourself, remember young Sam, and do try to laugh at yourself instead.

FRIDAY—FEBRUARY 22.

OUR friends Kevin and Heather went on an outing with their young family, one which included a journey on an old steam train.

They plunged into a tunnel halfway along the line, but whoever was responsible for switching on the carriage lights in the old-fashioned way had forgotten! They found themselves in total darkness; young Jamie squealed and began to cry.

"Don't be frightened," said Heather. "It's just a tunnel and it'll only be dark for a bit. There's light at the end, you know."

Wise words to remember at any time.

SATURDAY—FEBRUARY 23.

ON an "Open Garden Day" the Lady of the House and I went to see the snowdrop display, a small flower which inspired William Wordsworth to write "To A Snowdrop" — "nor will I then thy modest grace forget".

A light sprinkling of February snow sugared the ground, and the air was crisp and clear. In the garden we walked a little, and at first there were only a few clumps of white blooms here and there, but then we saw them . . . great drifts of those "Fair Maids Of February" carpeted the ground under the trees and down to the lake.

Heralds of Spring, they flowered in thin sunshine, and under the palest of blue skies. It was a sight to cheer the heart, a welcome reminder that not only Spring would soon be with us, but that late Winter has its beauties, too.

NOT A CLOUD
IN SIGHT

SUNDAY—FEBRUARY 24.

ANOTHER parable put he forth unto them, saying, The kingdom of heaven is likened unto a man which sowed good seed in his field.

Matthew 13:24

MONDAY—FEBRUARY 25.

OVER a century ago, these lines appeared in a local newspaper under the title "What Small Things Will Do:"

The smallest crust may save a human life;
The smallest act may lead to human strife;
The smallest touch may cause the body pain;
The smallest spark may fire a field of grain;
The smallest deed may tell the truly brave;
The smallest skill may serve a life to save;
The smallest drop the thirsty may relieve;
The slighest shock may make a heart to grieve.
Nought is so small that it may not contain
The rose of pleasure or the thorn of pain.

We don't know who wrote these words but they still pose quite a challenge for us today.

TUESDAY—FEBRUARY 26.

A BISHOP was preaching in a small country church when a boy began to fidget. After a while, his mother stood up to take him outside.

"It's quite all right," said the Bishop. "He isn't bothering me."

"I know," replied the mother. "But you're bothering him!"

WEDNESDAY—FEBRUARY 27.

THERE are many ways to keep things in proportion, just as there are dozens of little pieces of practical philosophy to remember and quote when we face what some people like to call "a bad day". One of my special favourites is this thought by an unknown author:

"Life will only come once, so make the most of it. God didn't give us all things to enjoy life, but life to enjoy all things".

THURSDAY—FEBRUARY 28.

THE Lady Of The House and I were choosing a selection of greetings cards one day, when I became a little distracted. In another part of the shop, I had found prayer cards and a display of bookmarks. Quite irresistible to me! Having paid for our purchases and finished our other shopping, we went home for a welcome refreshing cup of tea.

As she unpacked everything, the Lady of the House asked, "Who is the bookmark for, Francis?"

"For me," I replied a little sheepishly, as I didn't really need another one. However, when she read it, she understood why I had chosen it: "Faith is not believing that God can. It is knowing that He will".

I find comfort and pleasure in these words, and I'd like to pass them on to anyone who is in need of reassurance. Perhaps you, too, will be comforted by them.

March

HERE is a bouquet of thoughts for you, as fresh as the season they celebrate.

"There is no time like Spring,
When life's alive in everything."

Christina Rossetti.

"Spring in the world
And all things are made new."

Richard Hovey.

And who among us has not felt an uplift of heart and spirit in the delicious freshness of an early Spring morning, with all its promise of a new season to come?

LET me offer you some wise words entitled "I Did It My Way" which have been passed on to me by Beatrice Johnson:

To each of us, though rich or poor,
*   We have a common bond,*
And rugged pathways must endure
*   To reach the goal beyond.*
Just be yourself, you've much to give,
*   Perception as your tutor.*
Waste not your time, your hopes incline
*   Towards a better future.*

SUNDAY—MARCH 3.

BEWARE lest any man spoil you through philosophy and vain deceit, after the tradition of men, after the rudiments of the world, and not after Christ.

Colossians 2:8

MONDAY—MARCH 4.

A FRIEND who had been visiting Berlin for a short holiday was telling me what she had learned about the Wall that once divided that great city. "What a lot of misery and heartbreak would have been saved," she said, "if only they had built a bridge instead."

It's the same with all of us, isn't it? We put up walls to separate us from others in all sorts of ways when we should be building bridges of understanding.

Let us resolve to extend such a bridge towards friends, colleagues — and strangers — whenever we can.

TUESDAY—MARCH 5.

THESE lovely words were inscribed in an old Victorian Bible:

Within this sacred volume lies
The mystery of mysteries;
Oh, happiest thing of human race
To whom our God has given grace,
To hear, to read, to fear, to pray,
To lift the latch, to force the way.
But better had they ne'er been born
Who read to doubt, or read to scorn.

WEDNESDAY—MARCH 6.

IN spite of television and more recent innovations like the Internet, people seem to enjoy a good read just as much as ever. The historian Thomas Macaulay once said: "I would rather be a poor man in a garret with plenty of books than a rich man who does not like reading."

Sir William Robert Nicholl once told a large company of booksellers that he divided books into three categories — lovers, friends and acquaintances. Any booklover can probably make a similar claim. Even though our book friends have few new surprises in them, they often give rise to fresh thoughts or insights. And they can offer comfort in trouble.

We can turn to our books knowing they will enrich our lives.

THURSDAY—MARCH 7.

TOM had been working in the front garden all afternoon, so was a little discouraged to find, when he stood back, that his efforts were hardly noticeable.

Our friend Mary, passing by, saw his expression and laughed. "Oh, dear, Tom," she said. "You know, you shouldn't be downhearted just because you can't seem to make a huge difference right away. In fact, my grandmother always used to have a special saying: 'The State of Perfection is hard to reach, and the journey is best undertaken one step at a time'."

Mary's grandmother was a very wise woman!

FRIDAY—MARCH 8.

A FRIENDSHIP that is genuine
　Needs willingness to win it,
And genuine can help a lot
　For 'U' and 'I' are in it.
J. M. Robertson.

SATURDAY—MARCH 9.

IT was a cold, wet day, and we had just come home after the christening of little Sarah Louise, our friend's new baby granddaughter.

"I suppose it's rather silly of me, Francis," mused the Lady of the House, as we relaxed in front of the fire, "but whenever I go to a christening, it always makes me wonder what I would give a child, if I was a fairy godmother."

"Riches? Beauty?" I jokingly suggested.

"No," she replied firmly. "It would be the gift of being able to appreciate small pleasures. You know, we're often so busy wishing away our lives until the next big event — things like holidays, or special treats — that we quite forget to enjoy the simple day-to-day delights, such as good company, or a warm fire on a cold day. I do hope little Sarah Louise has many pleasures in her life but even more than that, I hope she will remember to cherish all of them."

SUNDAY—MARCH 10.

THIS is my commandment, That ye love one another, as I have loved you.
John 15:12

MONDAY—MARCH 11.

A PATCH of centuries-old herbs has sprung to life again in the grounds of Mount Grace Priory in North Yorkshire, which was closed during the Dissolution of the Monasteries in the reign of Henry VIII.

Since then, the seeds of weld which the monks used to dye their garments, and mullein which was used to make wicks for candles have lain dormant in the soil around the Priory. But when archaeological excavations were carried out, tons of soil were moved and spread around. Seeds which had been covered for centuries began to feel the sun again, the ancient herbs slowly began to grow and soon they stood six feet tall for all to see.

If we ever feel that our acts of kindness or offers of friendship have fallen on stony ground, then take heart. The passage of time alters most situations and we may well find that seeds we sowed have taken root, grown and borne fruit — just like those old monastery herbs.

TUESDAY—MARCH 12.

WE were discussing travels abroad many years ago when suddenly John, a good friend of ours, who has gained lots of experience via his own journeys through life, came up with a quotation which I've never forgotten:

"The most important journey any of us can make is the one where we meet people halfway."

"And it is often the most difficult," he added.

Keep these words in mind today.

WEDNESDAY—MARCH 13.

I WAS reminded one day through a chance encounter, that all of us at some time or another can be strangers in a strange land. There are so many situations in life that can make us so. Perhaps it is when we go into hospital, or when we are far from home separated from familiar faces and places; or it might even be that first working day in a new job, where we know nobody, and everything is strange.

So do not turn away when you encounter a stranger in a strange place. Smile, and speak that cheerful word of greeting, and ask, if appropriate, "Can I help you?" Help to make life easier for those who are strangers in a strange land.

THURSDAY—MARCH 14.

THE Lady of the House and I have a friend, Hannah, who has lived all her life in a small country village. Visiting while on a weekend break in the area, the Lady of the House and I caught sight of these words framed on her living-room wall:

Life is about who you love and who you hurt.
It's about who you make happy or unhappy.
It's about keeping or betraying trust.
Life is about not starting rumours and adding
*   to petty gossip.*
It's about stopping all jealousy, fear, ignorance,
*   and revenge.*
Most of all, though, Life is about spreading
*   true friendship.*

FRIDAY—MARCH 15.

A FRIEND of ours, Tim, was once on holiday in Wales. It had been very wet, so when the sun at last broke through and the clouds were skimming across the hilltops, he wrapped up well against the chilly breeze and ventured forth.

Walking up a hill, Tim saw a shepherd with his dog moving sheep from one fell to another. He stood and watched silently until the job was finished, marvelling at the work of both and their close bond.

"I've never been able to accept it before, Francis," he told me later, "how sheep know their shepherd and his voice, and that he knows them individually. They really do have such a close relationship — I've now seen it for myself, so I can believe it at last."

We fell silent as we thought of the sheep knowing their shepherd and of how he gently guides them.

SATURDAY—MARCH 16.

O F course it can be annoying when things don't go your way. When the pressure builds up, just remember two things:

Keep your temper. Nobody else wants it.

Keep your hair on. If you're a man, you may lose it soon enough!

SUNDAY—MARCH 17.

A ND he said, The things which are impossible with men are possible with God.

Luke 18:27

MONDAY—MARCH 18.

THERE are times, for all of us, when the sunshine of life seems to disappear. On such occasions — and let's hope they will be rare — I like to remind myself of these wise words by an unknown author:

Count your blessings instead of your crosses;
Count your gains instead of your losses.
Count your joys instead of your woes;
Count your friends instead of your foes.
Count your smiles instead of your tears;
Count your courage instead of your fears.
Count your full years instead of your lean;
Count your kind deeds instead of your mean.

Now, isn't there a great feeling of optimism and good cheer in thoughts such as these?

TUESDAY—MARCH 19.

OUR little church was completely full for the wedding of Ruth and Dennis. They were not a young couple but had found happiness together later in life and we were all sharing the happy occasion with them.

One of the wedding hymns was a modern one written by Bishop Timothy Dudley-Smith:

Lord, for the years your love has kept and guided,
Urged and inspired us, cheered us on our way.
Sought us and saved us, pardoned and provided:
Lord of the years, we bring our thanks today.

Lovely words for the couple's happy day — and ones that each one of us present could join in wholeheartedly.

MELLOW
YELLOW

WEDNESDAY—MARCH 20.

TO many people, having to go into hospital, especially for the first time, can be a daunting prospect. But if there is one great source of comfort, apart from the dedication of the medical staff, it is the friendly voice of hospital radio which can now be enjoyed in many hospitals.

Our friend Pauline was, for a time, a hospital radio presenter and she told me that it was one of the most worthwhile things she had ever taken part in. "To see patients' faces light up," she said, "when they hear a request especially for them and realise that their loved ones, friends, workmates and neighbours are thinking of them is such a tonic in itself."

Whatever their age, there is no time when people want to know others are thinking of them more than when they are unwell. So next time your local hospital asks for volunteers to help with their radio broadcasts, think about it. It is a most rewarding way to spend a few hours.

THURSDAY—MARCH 21.

I WOULD like to share with you this thought from the American poet and essayist Ralph Waldo Emerson:

"Although we travel the wide world over to find the beautiful, it is essential that we carry it with us or we find it not."

Take a few minutes to think about these words today — I am certain that you will find a great deal of truth in them.

FRIDAY—MARCH 22.

SPIRIT OF LIFE

I AM the waves on the ocean,
I am the sun on the sea,
I am the light in the morning,
I am the wind blowing free.
I am your strength in the darkness,
I am your laughter and mirth,
I am the joy of creation,
I am the pulse of the earth.

I am the life in all creatures,
I am each flower and tree,
I am the hope of tomorrow,
I am the things yet to be.
I am the noise of the city,
I am the peace on the fell,
I am your past and your future,
I am today — use it well!

Iris Hesselden.

SATURDAY—MARCH 23.

THE American writer Mark Twain had the gift of hitting on truths and expressing them in the most delightful way. He once said, "Always do right and you will please someone — and astonish the rest!"

SUNDAY—MARCH 24.

GOD is our refuge and strength, a very present help in trouble.

Psalms 46:1

MONDAY—MARCH 25.

LADY DAY, which falls on 25th March, is the Feast of the Annunciation of the Virgin Mary. In England it began the calendar year from 1155 to 1752 and it is still a quarter day.

As the mother of Christ, it was natural that flowers should be named after Mary, particularly those symbolising the Christian virtues of purity, humility and modesty. The delicate, white lily of the valley was named Our Lady's Tears and the shy violet was known as Our Lady's Modesty, while woodruff was called Our Lady's Lace.

In years gone by, the link between particular plants and worship was quite distinct and monks grew certain flowers with a religious association, not only to decorate churches but also as a focus for those who came to worship.

It is something we still do today. At Easter time churches are made beautiful with displays of daffodils and lilies to remind us once more of the resurrection of Christ and the promise of new life for all.

TUESDAY—MARCH 26.

HERE'S some good advice seen in the "Cleveland Ambulance N.H.T. Magazine":

Give me the ability to see
good things in the unforeseen places
And talents in unexpected people,
And O, Lord, give me the grace
to tell them so!

Suitable words for us all to bear in mind, surely.

WEDNESDAY—MARCH 27.

DO you ever buy "thank you" cards for family and friends? They come in many colourful designs and are suitable for many occasions.

I discovered one of these cards which really appealed to me. It was quite simple and only said: "Thank you for being there."

We all remember to thank others for gifts at birthday time and Christmas, but we don't always thank them for such things as their support and kindness. In times of worry we are fortunate to have true friends around. We should all remember to say to those who have shown care and concern: "Thank You For Being There".

THURSDAY—MARCH 28.

WHEN we see the wonderful displays of chocolate Easter eggs in the shops, it's difficult to believe that this custom has only been around for about one hundred years.

Traditional eggs were hard boiled and then brightly coloured. Some families even had their own secret dyes. Eggs have always been associated with Easter and the coming of Spring, a symbol of birth and resurrection. Egg rolling, which takes place in some parts of the country, is said to denote the rolling away of the stone from Christ's tomb. However we think of them, their bright boxes and cheerful wrappers announce that Winter is behind us and Spring is on the way.

Enjoy your Easter eggs, especially the chocolate ones!

UP THE
GARDEN
PATH

FRIDAY—MARCH 29.

WANT to make a change for the better? It's easy. The biggest room in the house is the room for improvement.

SATURDAY—MARCH 30.

ALL night long gale-force winds had been raging and shrieking around the house, and the Lady of the House and I feared for the garden. In the morning we looked out and saw that the plants were indeed blown about, even completely flattened in parts. Then my attention was caught by the distress of two birds in the branches of a damaged tree. Below the broken branches lay the ruins of their nest.

As I began to pick up some of the debris, I kept an eye on the unhappy birds; at first there was much frantic fluttering from branch to branch, every sign and sound one of panic. But then came a change — suddenly, it seemed, determined activity took over. The birds were beginning to rebuild their nest.

The loss of their nest must have come as a great shock, and yet perseverance coupled with hard work soon had the situation resolved. Now, that's an attitude we can all adopt.

SUNDAY—MARCH 31.

AND when they found not his body, they came, saying, that they had also seen a vision of angels, which said that he was alive.   Luke 24:23

April

MONDAY—APRIL 1.

THE Lady of the House and I once were walking along the Tissington Trail in the Peak District where many years ago the railway used to run. It was a sunny day in Spring and there was a lovely view for miles across the countryside, but to me the most beautiful thing of all was to see the wild flowers at the side of the path.

I picked a dandelion that was going to seed and blew across the top. We watched seeds blow away towards the fields.

As we stood there, I thought of how, nearly three hundred years ago, John and Charles Wesley wrote many words of comfort and joy which are still being sung and are helping people today.

Our own words and actions spread like seeds, too, and take root far beyond our sight or knowledge. Let us see that, like the Wesley brothers, they are words of kindness and love, which will have far-reaching results.

TUESDAY—APRIL 2.

" A REAL friend is the one who walks in when the rest of the world walks out."

Walter Winchell.

WEDNESDAY—APRIL 3.

TIME is too slow for those who wait,
Too swift for those who fear,
Too long for those who grieve,
Too short for those who rejoice.
But, for those who love,
Time is eternity.

Anon.

Spare a few moments today to think about these lines — I think you'll agree that they contain many worthwhile points to ponder.

THURSDAY—APRIL 4.

A NEW BEGINNING

EACH day is a new adventure,
Who knows what it may hold?
A voyage of discovery
With stories to unfold.
Who knows how many people
And places we may see?
How many new imaginings
Will help to set us free?

Each day brings opportunities
To journey far and wide,
Sometimes without a single step
Beyond our own fireside.
So always travel cheerfully,
Enjoying every mile,
Adventure in your heart and soul,
The journey is worthwhile!

Iris Hesselden.

FRIDAY—APRIL 5.

OUR friend Ethel lives a few streets away from us, and she quotes numerous little gems of advice passed on to her many years ago by her grandmother. Here is one of her sayings that particularly impressed us and which I'll now share with you:

"Never start a new day with the broken pieces of yesterday."

SATURDAY—APRIL 6.

DAFFODILS

*R**OUND** the corner before me lay*
Gold daffodils in full array
Circled 'neath the budding trees
Wafting gently in the breeze.

What a joy they bring to me —
Golden flowers and budding tree,
No fenced-off garden, or high wall
But growing open, free for all.

Nessie Gell.

SUNDAY—APRIL 7.

THE Lord our God be with us, as he was with our fathers; let him not leave us, nor forsake us: That he may incline our hearts unto him, to walk in all his ways, and to keep his commandments, and his statutes, and his judgments, which he commanded our fathers.

Kings 1 8:57-58

MONDAY—APRIL 8.

RYOKO KAWAGUCHI was a Japanese girl who was at a camp in the country when it began to snow, an unusual occurrence in her part of Japan. She caught a snowflake on the back of her hand and laid it gently on a rock before the warmth of her skin could melt it.

A reminder that beauty can be fleeting and should be appreciated whenever the opportunity arises.

TUESDAY—APRIL 9.

BORN in 1780, Mary Fairfax, later Mrs Mary Fairfax Greig Somerville, was a contemporary of the writer Jane Austen of "Pride And Prejudice" fame. Mary, the daughter of a naval officer, spent her childhood in Burntisland in Fife. She wanted to be as well educated as her brothers, and longed to study mathematics and science, something difficult to achieve at that time.

But Mary was both clever and determined and ignored objections to her studies. She became a famous scientific writer and mathematician. Somerville Hall, later College, was named in her honour, as was the Mary Somerville Scholarship For Women in mathematics at Oxford.

She would have agreed with Dr Samuel Johnson's words: "Nothing will ever be attempted, if all possible objections must be overcome."

By the way, Mary enjoyed Jane Austen's novels, and "thought them excellent", especially "Pride And Prejudice".

WEDNESDAY—APRIL 10.

A GOOD way of dealing with niggling worries which crop up from time to time is to write them down. Make a list of the things which are worrying you, just as you would write down a shopping list. Try to do it soon after breakfast, for early morning is often when worries seem most bothersome.

At the end of the day take a look at that list you so painstakingly wrote a few hours before. You'll probably find that not only did your worst fears come to little, but also the warmth of someone's unexpected kindness has left its glow.

Write it all down. You've nothing to lose — but your worries.

THURSDAY—APRIL 11.

SETTING yourself a specific course of action is surely something to be encouraged. In this context, I'm reminded of two famous people, a father and his son.

Sir Malcolm Campbell broke a world land speed record with his car "Bluebird" in 1935 and later, a world water speed record. Then his son Donald set up a classic water speed record in his turbo-jet hydroplane, also named "Bluebird", in Australia in 1964. Donald said that he cherished and adopted this advice from his famous father:

"To get ahead in life, set yourself a goal. Then, when you achieve it, set yourself another goal. And so on . . ."

Good advice for us all to keep in mind, surely.

FRIDAY—APRIL 12.

THE SPECIAL HOURS

I LOVE the early morning,
  When everything is still,
When every hour belongs to me,
  And I do as I will.

These special hours are precious,
  For they are just for me
To take and use them for myself,
  To create and be free.

The waking day surrounds me,
  And folds me in calm wings,
And gives me all the strength I need,
  To face what each day brings.
                    Chrissy Greenslade.

SATURDAY—APRIL 13.

HERE are two quotes about friendship to think about today:

"Friends are those rare people who ask how we are — and then wait to hear the answer."

"A good friend is one who neither looks down on you nor keeps up with you."

SUNDAY—APRIL 14.

HE that cometh from above is above all; he that is of the earth is earthly, and speaketh of the earth: he that cometh from heaven is above all.   John 3:31

MONDAY—APRIL 15.

A FRIEND of ours, Susan, came to visit on my birthday one year and presented me with a brightly-wrapped packet of Spring bulbs. Just to look at the packet brightened up a rather dismal wet day, and now each year our garden is so much brighter because of this thoughtful gift. The gift will continue to multiply, giving more and more blooms as the years go by.

Truly, it is always the thought that counts when choosing presents. Something apparently small and relatively insignificant can bring the greatest and most lasting pleasure.

TUESDAY—APRIL 16.

I T'S often said that the secret of success is hard work. Could that be why, for some, it's still a secret?

WEDNESDAY—APRIL 17.

THIS QUIET HOUR

D AYTIME draws towards its close,
Shadows steal across the sky;
Dusk now gathers in its cloak
Soft, lilac mists, and night owls cry.

A fragrance lingers in the air,
Enhanced by breezes on their way;
And in our thoughts to God, we add
Our thanks, for such a perfect day!

Elizabeth Gozney.

THURSDAY—APRIL 18.

A MONG the numerous thoughtful words which have been attributed to the 19th-century Swiss philosopher and critic Henri Frederic Amiel are these ones:

"Learn to limit yourself, to content yourself with some definite thing, and some definite work; dare to be what you are, and learn to resign with a good grace all that you are not, and to believe in your own individuality".

Isn't this wise and self-fulfilling advice for us all to take to heart?

FRIDAY—APRIL 19.

M Y friend Alex studied science at university and just can't drop the habit of classifying things into categories, frequently extending this to people. He was talking about this to me one day when we were remarking on the differences in folk we know.

He maintained that they could be broadly divided into two types. He said that he'd noticed that some on entering a room will say, "Ah, there you are!" On the other hand there are those who come in and exclaim proudly, "Here I am!"

It reminded me of a preacher who once said that at a public meeting there are those who are afraid they will be asked to speak. On the other hand, some will be afraid they will not be asked to speak.

How quickly a few words can reveal so much about us!

SATURDAY—APRIL 20.

ISN'T it so often the unexpected things in life which give the greatest pleasure? I'm thinking of those little surprises, such as small gifts or perhaps a few kind words.

We look forward to something for a long time, maybe a special occasion, only to be disappointed with the way things turn out. Yet an unexpected visit or phone call can bring back the sunshine into our lives.

If something cheerful and uplifting has happened to you or those closest to you, cherish it in your heart. You could then perhaps spare a thought for someone who would love to have a little surprise. You might put the sunshine back in their lives, too.

SUNDAY—APRIL 21.

HONOUR all men. Love the brotherhood. Fear God. Honour the king.

Peter I 2:17

MONDAY—APRIL 22.

ART BUCHWALD, the American writer, once said:

"I don't think yesterday was ever better than today. That's why I keep advising my friends not to wait ten years before admitting that today was 'great'."

Good advice, indeed. As are these words: "If you are hung up on nostalgia, you should just pretend that today really is yesterday — then go out and have a wonderful time!"

TUESDAY—APRIL 23.

WE were once privileged to share in a St George's Day service in magnificent Durham Cathedral. It was a special celebration and the pews were filled with young people. There were Scout troops, proudly displaying their banners; Cub packs, looking a little less confident; and tiny Beavers, in need of reassurance. It was a heart-warming experience, and not simply because the hymns were uplifting.

To see so many young people gathered together was wonderful, and it was as if the ancient stones were rejoicing at their presence. We hear so much about troublesome children and teenagers, so it is a joy to find there are many well-behaved and responsible young citizens. They certainly gave us and everyone present hope for the future.

God bless them all!

WEDNESDAY—APRIL 24.

TODAY may turn out to be trying — indeed it may already have been one of those periods in time that we would call "a bad day". At such times, I like to focus quietly on these wise words of comfort from Pope John XX111:

"Consult not your fears but your hopes and your dreams. Think not about your frustrations, but about your unfulfilled potential. Concern yourself not with what you tried and failed in, but with what it is still possible for you to do."

A time to put aside present setbacks and look with confidence to the new day called tomorrow.

THURSDAY—APRIL 25.

I WAS once thumbing through some books which a friend had given me after a stay in China. Among them I found a listing of some notable proverbs, including this one:

If you are planning for a year, sow rice,
If you are planning for a decade, plant trees,
If you are planning for a lifetime, educate a
person.

A worthy sentiment with which, I am sure, nobody — east, west, north or south — will disagree.

FRIDAY—APRIL 26.

THE Lady of the House and I agree whole-heartedly with these words, typed on an envelope we found between the covers of a tattered old book in a second-hand bookshop:

"We don't appreciate what we've got until we lose it, but we also don't appreciate what we've been missing until it arrives."

SATURDAY—APRIL 27.

HERE is a favourite saying from Norway, passed on to me by a friend who lives in the land of fjords and the midnight sun:

"On the path between the houses of friends, grass does not grow."

How charming a thought that is — and how true!

CLIMB EVERY MOUNTAIN

SUNDAY—APRIL 28.

NOW thanks be unto God, which always causeth us to triumph in Christ, and maketh manifest the savour of his knowledge by us in every place.

Corinthians II 2:14

MONDAY—APRIL 29.

I OFTEN browse through my old autograph album on rainy afternoons. In the space beside their signature some people have written a few lines, and these are always worth reading and recalling at a later date. Here's one example:

The world is wide.
In time and tide,
But God is guide,
That man is blest
Who does his best
And leaves the rest.

TUESDAY—APRIL 30.

I'M sure, like me, that you sometimes meet people who hesitate and wonder if they should tackle some new job or project. These words of advice by the poet and writer Edgar A. Guest are particularly apt:

There are thousands to prophesy failure;
*   There are thousands to point out the risks.*
But just buckle in with a bit of a grin,
*   Just take off your coat and go to it;*
Just start to sing as you tackle the thing,
*   That cannot be done and you'll do it.*

May

A THOUGHT for today from the pen of Robert Browning: "And after April, when May follows, and the whitethroat builds, and all the swallows".

Why, we are already on the threshold of Summer with all its long days and pleasures. The early 19th-century poet Thomas Hood wrote:

I remember, I remember,
The roses, red and white:
The violets and lily-cups,
Those flowers made of light!

Summer is a lovely season which beckons just around the corner.

WE hear all kinds of theories and tips these days as to how, in this modern world of instant communication, we should take more care over the often hasty comments that can be made in the heat of the moment.

I think the American humorist and philosopher Will Rogers Jr. got it right when he said: "Lead your life so you won't be ashamed to sell the family parrot to the town gossip".

Now, isn't that a tip worth following?

IN THE
DRIVING SEAT

FRIDAY—MAY 3.

ONE afternoon I turned up an encouraging little verse by the 19th-century American professor and writer Oliver Wendell Holmes, and gladly pass it on to you today:

There is no friend like the old friend who has shared our morning days, no greeting like his welcome, no homage like his praise:

Fame is the scentless sunflower with gaudy crown of gold; but friendship is the breathing rose, with sweets in every fold.

SATURDAY—MAY 4.

I WALKED out into the garden one morning and heard a bird singing its song of praise for another day. But try as I might, I couldn't see it, well hidden in a leafy branch. It reminded me of a proverb from China: "Keep a leafy branch in your heart and the singing bird will come."

Not so long ago that "leafy branch" had been bare, with no sign of life, completely inhospitable to any bird. But in a short time the branch was in full leaf, providing shelter.

In a broader context, this proverb encourages us to remember that better times will come again, no matter how difficult our present circumstances may be.

SUNDAY—MAY 5.

AND the glory of the Lord shall be revealed, and all flesh shall see it together: for the mouth of the Lord hath spoken it.   Isaiah 40:5

MONDAY—MAY 6.

THOSE who saw the film "The Secret Garden" based on the book by Frances Hodgson Burnett were surely inspired by the beautiful backdrop to the story. Its main theme was an inspiration in itself — how love and hope can overcome pain and sadness.

The author was born in the year 1849, not surrounded by magnificent gardens, but in the Cheetham Hill area of Manchester. Only after emigrating to the United States did she become a well-known writer and that, not surprisingly, took time.

Someone once asked her about the motive behind her writing. She did not quote either fame or money but replied, "I have tried to write more happiness into the world!" She would be astounded how her aim still succeeds today, I'm sure.

TUESDAY—MAY 7.

EVERY day brings its share of joys and disappointments. It might be something quite simple — perhaps the postman's delivery has included a bill that you had forgotten was due!

Then again, on a positive note you might receive a phone call from a friend who's delighted with news of a new arrival in the family. In the words of an observant old countryman I once met in the Lake District:

"It takes both the sun and the rain to make a rainbow."

WEDNESDAY—MAY 8.

A YOUNG neighbour, Jennie, was looking so happy one morning I was sure something good had happened. I was right.

"You know, I've been worried for some time about my son Ian and his baby brother," she said. "He seemed so jealous of the new baby, and I just didn't know what to do. Well, it's sorted itself!"

Ian regularly played a trick on his baby brother at the table, when he'd suddenly make a hideous grimace and begin to roar like a lion, straight at little Stewart. Jennie didn't know whether to punish Ian, and make him more resentful, or to comfort the baby, and still make him resentful.

Then, one lunchtime it happened — came the grimace and the roar, but instead of screams and tears Stewart himself made a hideous screwed-up face, and gave a loud and firm "Aaargh!" right back at Ian. A stunned silence followed, and then everyone burst out laughing.

I know the usual phrase is that a family who prays together stays together, but perhaps we should add: "a family who laughs together stays together".

THURSDAY—MAY 9.

THE ancient Greeks have given us many good words of advice, not least from the writer and philosopher Sophocles. One of his thoughts, apt for today, is this:

"One word frees us of all the weight and pain in life. That word is love."

FRIDAY—MAY 10.

A LITTLE love, a little trust,
A soft impulse, a sudden dream,
And life as dry as desert dust,
Is fresher than a mountain stream.

I think we all have experienced the truth of these lines. They were written by a man who was held in much affection by his fellow men of letters, the Irish writer and critic Stopford Augustus Brooke, who was born in 1832 in Letterkenny, Co. Donegal.

On the occasion of his 80th birthday, his fellow writers sent him birthday wishes with much goodwill. In reply, Stopford Brooke sent them his beautiful paraphrase of the 23rd Psalm embodying his faith.

SATURDAY—MAY 11.

DO you ever mislay things? If you are at all like me, then I'm sure you do!

The Lady of the House made me smile one day when she said, "Cheer up, Francis," as I was trying to locate a book I'd had a moment before. "After all, there's only one thing that you can be quite certain of finding the very moment you start looking for it."

"What's that?" I asked curiously.

She laughed. "Fault — and you wouldn't want to find that, would you?"

No, indeed, I think I would prefer to be the sort of person who sometimes loses a book, rather than one who is always finding fault!

SUNDAY—MAY 12.

O GIVE thanks unto the Lord, for he is good: for his mercy endureth for ever.

Chronicles I 16-34

MONDAY—MAY 13.

MOST of us have our dreams and our ambitions. Each time we perhaps start to laugh at some of them, I'm reminded of the country blacksmith from Keir Mill, in Dumfriesshire, who first thought up the idea of riding along on two wheels without touching the ground.

Kirkpatrick Macmillan, who died in 1878, was nicknamed "Daft Pate" for daring to think a pedal-driven bicycle was possible. Even friends and neighbours who respected him laughed at his idea, and were amazed when he rode the 70-mile journey to Glasgow in two days in June 1842. He beat the Carlisle to Glasgow mail coach on that history-making ride.

So never scoff at someone else's ideas and aspirations, however far-fetched they appear. Remember, some dreams do come true.

TUESDAY—MAY 14.

LUCK plays a part in all our lives. It's often a very welcome help, but of course we can't rely on it. In this connection, I have never forgotten a piece of advice given to me years ago:

"If your luck isn't what it should be, put a 'p' in front of it".

WEDNESDAY—MAY 15.

SIMON Weston is well known as a man who recovered from horrific burns after being injured during the Falklands War in 1982. He has since sought to give to young people what has become known as the Weston Spirit.

He now admits that his injuries were, in a sense, a blessing because of the positive aspects of life that he has experienced in the years since *Sir Galahad* was hit. Simon spends most of his time raising money for the Weston Spirit Charity. This seeks to help young people from inner cities to develop their potential, to teach them the art of trust and respect, and to understand the meaning of community spirit and reconciliation, exemplified in Simon Weston's own contact with the Argentinian pilots who were once his enemies.

They have shared a lot of tears, but a lot of laughter, too, and realised that life really is worth living. They bear no grudges, and in fact have become good friends.

All this came about because Simon Weston was prepared to extend a friendly hand, open his heart and share in someone else's pain and heartache.

THURSDAY—MAY 16.

"LET there be kindness in your face, in your eyes and in the warmth of your greeting. For children, for the poor, for all who suffer and are alone, always have a happy smile. Give them not only your care, but your heart."

Mother Teresa.

FRIDAY—MAY 17.

*I*F *I could make a special gift,*
  This gift I'd give to you,
I'd take a golden Summer's day,
  A morning fresh and new.
I'd fill this day with fragrance,
  The perfume of a rose,
Then tie this gift with rainbows
  And love which grows and grows.
I'd fill a basket with the stars
  To shine for you each night,
To make your world a special place
  Of wonder and delight.
I'd scatter sunbeams on your path
  And warm each breeze that blows,
Yet all I have is gifts of love —
  But this love grows and grows!

Iris Hesselden.

SATURDAY—MAY 18.

TWO wise thoughts for you to ponder on today:

You are wise if you know when to speak your mind and when to mind your speech.

You are wise if you know the difference between keeping your chin up and sticking your neck out.

SUNDAY—MAY 19.

PRAISE ye the Lord: for it is good to sing praises unto our God. Psalms 147:1

MONDAY—MAY 20.

I LIKE the story I heard about John Paton who brought Christianity to the people of the Pacific Islands and taught them about the love of God.

Years later when Communists arrived, they told the islanders, "There is no God. You have listened to fables and lies."

"Well," retorted the Chief, "you should thank the God you do not believe in, for if you had arrived before Paton, we would have eaten you."

TUESDAY—MAY 21.

THERE is nothing more pleasing than a lovely garden with flowers to grace each season. It is a marvel that everything we see starts life as tiny seeds. In "The African Prayer Book" by Archbishop Desmond Tutu, these words from the pen of Harry Alfred Wiggett reflect this beautifully:

I did not hear you fall
From pod to Mother Earth,
I did not hear you call
Or cry your humble birth.
I did not hear you sigh
As silently you grew,
I did not hear a why
Because God made you.
And yet your silence spake
Of confidence and might,
And purpose as you broke
Through earth into the light.

<u>WEDNESDAY—MAY 22.</u>
HIGH AND LOWS
WORRY and confusion are seldom far away,
If pessimistic notions are allowed to win
the day.
It isn't always easy, but at least it's worth a try —
Keep aggravation at a low, and hopes upon
a high.

J. M. Robertson.

<u>THURSDAY—MAY 23.</u>

PRIDE of place among eight-year-old Katie's birthday presents was a toy vanity case. "I must have time to put on my make-up," she said in an adult voice when party time drew near.

So Katie carefully laid out the tiny jars and face powder compact, lipstick, eyebrow pencil and cotton-wool pack. Peering closely into the mirror on the lid, she began . . . Cream was scooped from one jar, carefully smoothed on, then wiped off; next came colour from another jar, then a dusting of powder, followed by a careful application of lipstick. Finally, her eyebrows were meticulously brushed.

No-one had taught Katie the art of make-up. She was simply copying what her mother did, and had obviously noted everything in great detail. Her mother was her model, as are parents everywhere — and all adults, for that matter. What a privilege we carry through life, and what a responsibility, too!

FRIDAY—MAY 24.

A MINISTER had grown old in the service of his church and things had got rather out of hand. The building itself needed a Spring clean and a lot of small repairs were required. Then the churchyard was waist high in weeds with grass and ivy growing over the tombstones, while paths were thick with dandelions.

Then a new, younger man was appointed. He had a charming wife and six children. In no time he had worked out a rota and each child was given an allotted task. In a matter of weeks the whole place was sparkling bright — pews and pulpit polished, brasses cleaned and carpets regularly swept. The congregation, seeing such industry, joined in eagerly — in the churchyard the weeds disappeared and tombstones were cleared.

When people expressed their appreciation the minister said, "Well, every little helps and then the job is soon done." How true! Each contribution may have been small but was necessary to complete the whole task, as well as giving encouragement to others.

SATURDAY—MAY 25.

I'D like to share with you today these words which come from an old proverb much repeated among the Cherokee Indians:

"When you were born, you cried and the world rejoiced. Live your life so that when you die, the world will cry — and you will rejoice."

SUNDAY—MAY 26.

FOR where two or three are gathered together in my name, there am I in the midst of them.

Matthew 18:20

MONDAY—MAY 27.

GRACE is newly retired, and when the Lady of the House and I visited her, we found her in old clothes, her face dust-streaked, energetically turning out her attic. Boxes and plastic sacks were stacked in her hall which was full of useful bits and pieces destined for Grace's favourite good causes and charity shops.

"I'm almost finished," she said to us with a smile. "Let's have a cup of tea."

When we were comfortably seated, our friend went on to say, "Next I am going to tackle another overdue job — I am going to Spring clean my routine, and stop doing quite a few things!"

Maybe we looked a little startled but we listened carefully to what Grace had to say. "You see," she explained, "in recent years I've got into the habit of doing certain things, which either don't need to be done, or can be done by someone else — for example, committees benefit from new members with fresh ideas."

Grace then told us that with her extra free time she intended to do things she had long promised herself she would do. Shakespeare sums up such a situation aptly:

"Superfluous branches we lop away, that bearing boughs may live."

TUESDAY—MAY 28.

I NEVER seem to tire of reading the books by Richard Jeffries, a great naturalist who communicated his love of nature through his vivid style of writing. He died at an early age in 1887, and although his last years were a constant struggle against ill-health, he wrote some classic nature books. "Amaryllis At The Fair" is probably the best-known one.

On re-reading Jeffries' "Pageant Of Summer" I was struck by this sentence which sums up his philosophy and love of nature: "My heart is fixed firm and stable in the belief that ultimately the sunshine and the Summer, the flowers and the azure sky, shall become as it were, interwoven into man's existence; he shall take from all their beauty and enjoy their glory."

That seems to me to express in a nutshell the truth that man is inextricably bound with nature; a source of beauty which enriches life.

WEDNESDAY—MAY 29.

"WE took our grandson David to church one Sunday," said our friend Jane, "and as one of the congregation walked to the lectern to read the first lesson, he watched closely. When the reader opened the big lectern Bible, young Dave opened his eyes wide in horror . . . "Gran, he's not going to read all that, is he?"

I joined in the laughter, sympathising with that little fellow's first impression — those lectern Bibles are massive-looking volumes, after all.

<u>THURSDAY—MAY 30.</u>

MICHELLE, who works in a hairdressing salon was getting married and everyone heard lots about all the preparations — the bridesmaids' dresses, wedding cake, church music and so on.

As the date of the wedding approached, the Lady of the House remarked, "I expect you can hardly wait for the big day, Michelle."

"Well, yes and no," she replied. "When that day comes I shall be the happiest girl on earth, but these last few weeks have been terrific. All my family and friends have done such wonderful things for me and it has been a really special time."

What a worthwhile pattern for life — to enjoy to the full the good things that each day brings without losing any of the anticipation of what is just around the corner.

<u>FRIDAY—MAY 31.</u>

A LIFETIME will bring so many different experiences our way — in fact, it's not possible to remember each and every one. But we usually remember the good ones, no matter how long ago they were.

In this context, we should think about these words by former First Lady of the USA, Mrs Eleanor Roosevelt:

"Many people will walk in and out of your life, but only true friends will leave footprints in your heart."

June

SATURDAY—JUNE 1.

THE Lady of the House and I watched a television programme about old churches and found it very interesting. The person being interviewed referred to them as "spiritual banks", where she was able to make a withdrawal when feeling rather low.

We thought this a very apt description as we have often felt revived even after a short visit. The magnificent cathedrals of Durham, Wells and Salisbury immediately spring to mind, but there are many smaller churches where we can discover peace and tranquillity, places where the centuries of prayer and meditation have created a wonderful atmosphere.

Perhaps we can't always visit as often as we would like, but we can certainly travel there in thought. If you have discovered your own "spiritual bank", I hope it gives you that inner peace we all need.

SUNDAY—JUNE 2.

AND, behold, I send the promise of my Father upon you: but tarry ye in the city of Jerusalem, until ye be endued with power from on high.

Luke 24:49

MONDAY—JUNE 3.

ONE afternoon, I went with friends to visit the garden belonging to one of their elderly neighbours. Bert showed me round with great pride and it seemed that almost every plant had some memory attached to it — a friend who had moved away; a friend who wanted to share his abundant crop of seedlings; and then one who had succeeded in raising plants from difficult-to-grow seeds.

What a worthwhile garden that was — full of friends of beloved memory.

TUESDAY—JUNE 4.

DO You have a minute, Lord,
In this busy, noisy day?
Just a minute You can spare
To listen, when I pray.
Often I am troubled, Lord,
So many things to do,
I know I will find guidance
If I can talk to You.

The universe is vast, Lord,
And wonderful to see,
The world is filled with people
And yet, You notice me.
If You have a minute, Lord,
Just one to set apart,
I'll listen for Your answer
And hear You, in my heart.

Iris Hesselden.

WEDNESDAY—JUNE 5.

"WHY isn't Grandma getting up?" the five-year-old asked his mother. "It's a lovely morning and she's missing it."

Grandma smiled as she heard this remark outside her bedroom door. She was quite aware of the beautiful day and the sun peeping through the curtains, but she felt a little tired after the previous day's journey. However, she called to her daughter and grandson, and they came to sit on her bed to discuss her visit and what they'd all do together.

It was a few days later and back in her own home, when she recalled these words and thought about their significance. How often we take for granted the beauty and wonders of nature! She resolved to start each day as though it were a great adventure.

Perhaps we should all do the same. Then we can truthfully say that we are not missing the lovely morning, or the sunshine!

THURSDAY—JUNE 6.

ONE evening I phoned a friend I hadn't been in touch with for a while. "Oh, hello!" he said. "Now, I have been thinking about you and have been meaning to call." We were soon chatting away like old times but the conversation had got off to a sticky start because we'd both been guilty of putting off contacting each other.

I've now memorised an apt saying: "Don't just think about it — do it."

FRIDAY—JUNE 7.

I CAUGHT sight of these words framed above the desk of a friend:

"A man may die, nations may rise and fall, but an idea lives on for all time."

Words that are surely well worth remembering. They were spoken by one of the world's most distinguished statesmen, John F. Kennedy, former President of the United States Of America.

SATURDAY—JUNE 8.

IT was just an old horseshoe. There it lay, barely visible among the soil where the plough had unearthed it, a reminder of an age when horses worked the land. I retrieved it from the furrow and, once home, put it in the garden shed.

Not long afterwards, when our friends Philip and Rosemary announced that they were to be married, I tried to think of an unusual present for them. After much thought, the old horseshoe came to mind.

For several days, working on the horseshoe became almost a labour of love for me, as earth and rust were painstakingly removed to reveal the blacksmith's creation in its former glory. My decision to paint the horseshoe silver truly transformed it, and later I looked at my handiwork with pleasure.

Philip and Rosemary were delighted when they received the silver-coloured horseshoe on their wedding day. I couldn't have chosen a better present, they said, a token of our love for them.

SUNDAY—JUNE 9.

BLESSED are the merciful: for they shall obtain mercy.

Matthew 5:7

MONDAY—JUNE 10.

A FRIEND who works in a library sent me these lines which she came across, and I'd like to share them with you today:

Give me enough tears to keep me human,
Enough humour to keep me wise,
Enough setbacks to keep me humble,
Enough accomplishments to keep me
confident,
Enough patience to teach me waiting,
Enough hope to teach me trusting,
Enough friends to give me love,
Enough memories to give me comfort.

TUESDAY—JUNE 11.

TODAY, like so many others throughout the year, will probably bring you a mixture of things both good and not so good. But whatever today brings your way, I'm sure that you will manage to cope with those moments which may disappoint and find pleasure in others which are brighter.

Taking things in our stride is rather like the advice contained in this little-known saying: "You cannot prevent the birds of sorrow from flying over your head, but you can prevent them from building nests in your hair."

WEDNESDAY—JUNE 12.

WE were on a sponsored walk one Saturday and in our party was a father and his young son. At one point on the route the path rose steeply — a real climb lay ahead. Would the little lad manage it, I wondered?

His father strode on ahead and, with an encouraging smile, stretched out his hand to the boy and pulled him on and upwards.

This is surely a parable of life. If someone needs help to overcome an obstacle, you don't stand back and make sympathetic noises — you go in front and stretch out a helping hand.

THURSDAY—JUNE 13.

ONE Saturday our friend, Jane, visited a stately home with friends from her church. They were all impressed with the gardens which were beautifully set out with carefully-mowed lawns and wonderful flowers.

Next morning, the vicar brought a large bunch of bluebells into the church. During his sermon he told his congregation, "It was a good day out yesterday — what wonderful flowers we saw, each looking perfect. Well, we're like flowers, but not like the ones we saw. We're more like these!" He held up some of the bluebells, one at a time.

"This one's a bit windswept, this one's a bit faded and this one looks well past its best. Yes, we're just like flowers, not perfect ourselves, but just put us together. . ." He held up the whole bunch. "And we can light up the world!"

FRIDAY—JUNE 14.

SLIGHT DIFFERENCE

THE rich man arrived at the bank to inquire,
"How much am I worth? Let me know."
The manager sighed, and on checking replied,
"It must be ten million or so."

The same man arrived up in Heaven to ask,
"How much am I worth? Make it clear."
But he didn't expect to be told with effect,
"You're no different from anyone here."

J. M. Robertson.

SATURDAY—JUNE 15.

HERE are some thoughtful words from my book of jottings. They are by no means modern, but seem just as appropriate for us today as when they were first written:

"Happiness is a butterfly which, when pursued, is always just beyond your grasp, but which, if you sit down quietly, may alight upon you."

Nathaniel Hawthorne.

"Never be ashamed to own you have been in the wrong: 'tis but to say that you are wiser today than you were yesterday."

Jonathan Swift.

SUNDAY—JUNE 16.

FEAR thou not; for I am with thee.

Isaiah 41:10

MONDAY—JUNE 17.

WHEN he was twenty-five years old William Wilberforce travelled abroad, accompanied by the clergyman Isaac Milner. They not only enjoyed the sights and sounds of foreign lands, but found time to study the Old Testament in Greek and also discussed the Christian faith and conditions, including slavery.

Wilberforce entered Parliament soon after his return and began to campaign against the slave trade. Many supported this worthy cause, yet it took years of patience and struggle to stop this trade in human misery. Wilberforce never ceased his endeavours, while Isaac Milner's faith and support often enabled him to carry on the campaign.

A visit to William Wilberforce's house in Hull brings much of his life and work back to mind. There sits a statue of the famous campaigner who looks as if he is watching his visitors who are recalling his anti-slavery campaign and all it achieved for mankind.

TUESDAY—JUNE 18.

YOUTH is impetuous. It always has been and always will be. I remember when I was a young man I was taught a valuable lesson. I had made a hasty decision and then realised it had been a mistake.

"You see," said the older and wiser man, "going fast is no advantage unless you're going in the right direction."

WEDNESDAY—JUNE 19.

OUR friend Robert visited us one morning and he was happy to pass on to the Lady of the House and me these two thoughts:

"It is a wise move to be planning your future while you also live one day at a time."

"Be sure to learn from yesterday, live for today, and hope for tomorrow."

THURSDAY—JUNE 20.

THERE is a Chinese saying: "Thank you for supplying coal in the snowy weather", which actually means, "Thank you for helping out in a moment of need." It is something most of us have had cause to be grateful for and reflects the New Testament admonition: "Be doers of the world and not merely hearers."

Jimmy Carter, a former president of the United States, is a practising Christian. As well as teaching in Sunday School, he put his faith into action in practical ways as a "doer" and peacemaker. George Hamilton IV, the Country and Western singer, once said of him, "Do you know what he is doing? He is up a ladder with hammer and nails making homes for the homeless." Then he added, "He really walks his talk."

It is not an expression I had heard before then, but it says it all. I hope you will join me in adopting it and if there is someone we know who is in need today, let's see if we can do something to help at once — after all, tomorrow may be too late.

FRIDAY—JUNE 21.

HERE is a toast I particularly like — it says so much in a few well-chosen words: "Love to one, friendship to a few, and goodwill to all."

SATURDAY—JUNE 22.

OVER 200 years ago, a musician and his two children travelled to Vienna. The little girl's dress had worn very thin, and her brother asked: "If we make some money in the city, Father, you'll buy my sister a new dress, won't you?"

Father didn't know what to do. He expected that all the money he had would be needed to pay the customs duty on his harp and to buy food. When he reached the customs office, the inspector examined the harp and named a large sum for the duty. Before any money could change hands, the six-year-old boy picked up the harp and started playing music which entranced all within earshot.

"I've never heard anything as beautiful as this before. Play again, my boy," said the official. And, as the youngster continued to play, the officer told his father: "Put your money away — I'll pay the duty. Your lad deserves some encouragement."

The boy immediately said to his father that he could now buy Marianne a dress, and nobody was more delighted when Marianne wore her new gown at a concert the family gave in Vienna. Over the next 30 years "the little sorcerer" produced some unforgettable music, including "The Marriage Of Figaro" and "The Magic Flute" — his name was Wolfgang Amadeus Mozart.

THE FRIENDSHIP BOOK

SUNDAY—JUNE 23.

AND Jesus returned in the power of the Spirit into Galilee: and there went out a fame of him through all the region round about.
                                                              Luke 4:14

MONDAY—JUNE 24.

DID you know that on the wall at the entrance to the United Nations H.Q. in New York are engraved these words from the Old Testament: "They shall beat their swords into ploughshares, and their spears into pruning forks." Do you also know that within that great building, teeming with people of all nationalities, is a Meditation Room? In this room is a plaque with words written by Dag Hammarskjöld, the Swedish Internationalist who was Secretary of the United Nations for seven years:

This is a room devoted to peace
And those who are giving their lives for peace.
This is a room of quiet where only
Thoughts should speak.

TUESDAY—JUNE 25.

OLD GEORGE was getting out his lawnmower as I passed one lovely morning when his flowers and shrubs were looking their very best.

"Beautiful day!" I called over the hedge.

"Yes," he replied. "God's creation is wonderful. But I just wish he had made slower-growing grass!"

FLOWER
POWER

WEDNESDAY—JUNE 26.

WHEN our friend Mary first found an old book during a holiday, it seemed of little significance. There it lay in an attic gathering dust but the title "Heart Echoes" caught her attention and impelled her to open its pages.

Not only had she stumbled upon a treasure in verse but its author, she discovered, was someone whose name had been forgotten, William Robertson, born in 1833. He was a humble clerk who found inspiration for his work in his village, Bankfoot in Perthshire. He was later laid to rest in the local churchyard in 1891.

Mary found his headstone close to a path. The simple inscription told of his passing, that he was a poet and yet for years he had remained unknown.

William Robertson never achieved fame and fortune — perhaps it was never his intention to do so. As the title of the book which Mary found suggests, he indeed wrote from the heart. And now, in our own time, he continues to touch the hearts of others.

THURSDAY—JUNE 27.

THE Lady of the House drew my attention to this tip she found while thumbing through the pages of a women's magazine:

"There is a facelift you can perform yourself that is guaranteed to improve your whole appearance. It is called a smile."

Now, there's a beauty tip for us all that doesn't cost anything!

FRIDAY—JUNE 28.

PEOPLE who don't talk about their activities — or their good deeds — always leave me quite humbled. And so I was delighted to come across this definition of the word generosity:

"Real generosity is doing something nice for someone who will never find out".

Doing someone a good deed doesn't have to be something you tell the world about!

SATURDAY—JUNE 29.

THE Lady Of The House and I were lucky enough to attend a play put on by a local school. The acting was not quite of Oscar-winning standard, and many of the players needed a prompt or two — but, oh, the pleasure they took in their performance!

As the curtain came down to heartfelt applause, it occurred to me just what a wonderful quality enthusiasm is. Not only can it turn a tiny glow into a brilliant blaze, it also lights up the life of all who come into contact with it.

Watching the children take their well-deserved bow, it struck me that many adults might have learned a thing or two that evening.

SUNDAY—JUNE 30.

AND in every work that he began in the service of the house of God, and in the law, and in the commandments, to seek his God, he did it with all his heart, and prospered.   Chronicles II 31:21

July

<u>MONDAY—JULY 1.</u>

HELEN is a young lady with a sweet tooth but when she found it difficult to get into her Summer dresses, she decided to cut down on cakes and chocolate. Consequently, her friends were surprised when she turned up at the office one day with a large chocolate gateau.

"We thought you were giving up all that kind of thing," they said.

"Well, I prayed about it," Helen said, "and I'm sure God game me a sign that it would be all right to eat this gateau. I said, 'Lord, if you want me to have that cake, let there be a parking space right outside the shop.' And on the eighth time round the block, there was!"

<u>TUESDAY—JULY 2.</u>

THOMAS EDISON is often remembered for his persistence despite disappointments at various times in his life. Some years after his death in 1931, his desk was opened and among the papers was a card bearing the following admonition:

"When down in the mouth, remember Jonah. He came out all right!"

That's encouragement enough for any of us!

WEDNESDAY—JULY 3.

L IFE'S worth living surely,
  If one cares to look around
And ascertain the many
  Fine reasons that abound;
Blessings can be counted,
  And, by their presence, giving
An estimate of just how much
  That life is worth the living.

J. M. Robertson.

THURSDAY—JULY 4.

ON a lovely Summer's day, the Lady of the House and I visited our friends Jim and Rosemary in their new home. I think we looked just a trifle puzzled when, after we had all walked round the garden, Rosemary suggested that we should come and see her "Quiet Corner".

We followed her upstairs, and there it was — a landing at the very top of the house with a miniature bow window overlooking the garden, and beyond, the distant hills. A sewing basket sat on the floor, and an open book lay on the seat of a comfortable old armchair. It was very peaceful.

"This is my Quiet Corner," Rosemary said. Then she added with a smile, "Sometimes Jim borrows it! It's a special place where we can sit quietly, relax and let the world go by."

The Lady of the House and I nodded in understanding. Quiet moments are infinitely precious in this busy world. We all need them, don't you agree?

FRIDAY—JULY 5.

PERHAPS someone has irked you ever so slightly today? Maybe someone forgot to say "thank you" for a favour you did yesterday. Or did a neighbour make a remark that wasn't too kind about a mutual friend?

When little things start to make you more "edgy" than usual, think about these words: "Deal with the faults of others as gently as with your own."

SATURDAY—JULY 6.

THESE words were written by a disabled person, but don't you think there is a message here for each one of us?

Blessed are you who take time to listen to difficult speech, for you help me to know that if I persevere I can be understood.

Blessed are you who never ask me to hurry up, or take my tasks from me, for often I need time rather than help.

Blessed are you who ask for my help, for my greatest need is to be needed.

Blessed are you who, with a smile, encourage me to try again.

Blessed are you who respect me and love me just as I am.

SUNDAY—JULY 7.

FOR other foundation can no man lay than that is laid, which is Jesus Christ.   Corinthians I 3:11

THE FRIENDSHIP BOOK

MONDAY—JULY 8.

WE all need a holiday, a time to relax, to forget daily routine, to see new places, meet new people, to enjoy a change for a week or two either at home or abroad. When we are away what becomes our main priority, apart from the obvious things like sun cream, taking photographs and sightseeing? Yes, I am thinking of postcards.

It is when we are away that we think of family, friends, workmates and neighbours, and how we enjoy browsing through the vast range of colourful scenes to pick that particular view for each person on our list. Then we think of the appropriate words to write in each card's limited space.

It's good to get away but wherever we travel there is always time to think of others and that is the beauty of this Victorian invention — family and friends are kept in touch across the miles.

TUESDAY—JULY 9.

FOR many of us, schooldays meant time spent in the classroom learning the basis of what were once known as "The Three Rs" — reading, writing and 'rithmetic, all very important subjects.

A friend, Rob, has now told me of another set of three Rs:

Respect for self,
Respect for others,
Responsibility for your actions.

I think you will agree that these can be just as valuable in their own way.

WEDNESDAY—JULY 10.

I WONDER if you know these words? "Love is a proud and gentle thing, a better thing to own than all the wide impossible stars . . ."

More than a quarter of a century has passed since I first read them as a quotation; the author wasn't given. I have never forgotten them. Love gives a golden warmth to life, and it is not only a blessed thing to receive but to give — there is never too much love in the world.

THURSDAY—JULY 11.

THE Lady of the House and I always enjoy going to the Summer fête held by our church. One year, we happened to bump into Stella, who was beaming as brightly as the sunshine outside. She confided happily that she had just won first prize for the best home-made cake.

After congratulating her, the Lady of the House was eager to know the secret of the winning recipe. Stella laughed. "The most important ingredient is perseverance!" she said. "I've been entering the competition for years now, and was often disappointed at not winning a prize. But every time I felt like giving up, I remembered that old motto, 'If at first you don't succeed . . .' So I kept on trying, and now I'm very glad that I did."

I couldn't help but think that Stella's greatest victory lay not so much in winning, but in her recognition of the importance of never losing hope.

FRIDAY—JULY 12.

*O*FFER *to fetch,*
Offer to carry,
Offer to lend a hand.
Offer to listen,
Offer to stay,
Offer time
To understand.
                    Jean Harris.

SATURDAY—JULY 13.

AT one time signposts were only erected at crossroads, but nowadays there are lesser members of the signpost family to be seen. These are the black and gold finger posts in many towns and villages which indicate what to see and where to go to find it. Some finger posts are in foreign languages, like the ones in Japanese at Howarth, a very popular place with visitors from that part of the world.

Oliver Wendell Holmes, the great American writer, pointed out: "The greatest thing in the world is not so much where we stand as in which direction we are moving."

How true that is — when it comes to both sightseeing and life.

SUNDAY—JULY 14.

I WILL not leave you comfortless: I will come to you.

                                        John 14: 18

MONDAY—JULY 15.

THERE are few things in life so final as the sound of a door that has just slammed. Maybe a strong gust of wind has been the cause. Or perhaps a friend or family member has fled the room in a momentary burst of temper.

When a door closes, I like to remind myself that it will not stay that way for ever. Often there is another door that will open at the most unexpected moment. I'm reminded of these words of wisdom which the Lady of the House found inside the pages of an old autograph album:

"When the door of happiness closes, another opens. Just remember, never keep gazing so long at the closed door that you don't see the one that is opening for you."

TUESDAY—JULY 16.

I HAVE always loved the simple pleasure on country rambles of following the winding course of a river through meadow, hill and valley, forever on an eternal journey during which it will change character. Majestic waterfalls, rushing rapids, linked by a small river, will change in mood and the weather also plays its part.

Always there is the unexpected along the way — perhaps a silent pond, a haven of peace where the clouds are reflected and wild flowers grow in colourful clumps along the banks. On a sunny day what can be better than to unwind in a peaceful spot, surrounded by the beauties of nature, all worries receding far into the distance.

WEDNESDAY—JULY 17.

*I*T'S *never easy to be glad*
When all around is gloom.
It's never easy to prevent
What pessimists may groom.
It's never easy to put right
What's wrong as time goes by,
Although it's never easy
At least it's worth a try.
J.M. Robertson.

THURSDAY—JULY 18.

NINE-YEAR-OLD James decided to clear out some of his toys, including those he considered were now too young for him. Among his discarded playthings were a number of soft animals and teddies.

His mother, being older and wiser, urged him not to be too hasty. There was one big teddy which had been a favourite and even James, on reflection, felt he couldn't part with it. But he made sure that he hid the teddy at the bottom of the toy box, just in case his friends happened upon it!

A few weeks later, he wasn't feeling very well and went to bed early. When his mother looked in later, she was surprised to see the big teddy lying beside James, both snugly tucked in for the night.

She smiled to herself and thought, we are never too old for teddies. After all, didn't she still have one of her own sitting patiently in the spare room, waiting for her to say "Goodnight"?

THE FRIENDSHIP BOOK

FRIDAY—JULY 19.

OUR young friends Ann and Bill decided that their dining-room was badly in need of a facelift. However, before the serious business of painting and papering could begin, things had to be moved.

The shelves were cleared of books, CDs and videos, the cupboards emptied and everything taken out into the hall. Finally, the curtains and blinds were removed.

We rang to see how things were progressing and were told it looked quite dreadful. "Your cat won't like it!" I laughingly remarked.

"She doesn't," Ann told me, quite seriously. "She keeps coming in and out wearing a mournful face."

I thought this was a lovely description and it made me realise that animals have feelings, too. Luckily, everything turned out well in the end — pretty wallpaper and borders, plus a freshly-painted ceiling. Ann tells me that the purring of the cat can now be heard even in the next room!

SATURDAY—JULY 20.

WHAT, I've often asked myself, are the best as well as the most beautiful things in the world? A wise old gentleman had the right idea and the right interpretation, as I remember from a chance encounter many years ago.

He told me, "The best and the most beautiful things in this world cannot be seen or even touched. They must be felt with the heart."

SUNDAY—JULY 21.

AND ye shall take you on the first day the boughs of goodly trees, branches of palm trees, and the boughs of thick trees, and willows of the brook; and ye shall rejoice before the Lord your God seven days.

Leviticus 23:40

MONDAY—JULY 22.

KATHLEEN Gillum's poem "Grandchild" will strike a chord with all grandparents:

You came a year ago today
And made your presence felt,
Every time we look at you
Our hearts begin to melt.
You're such a precious, special child,
Blonde hair and big blue eyes,
You wind us round your fingers
Even at your tiny size.
I wish for you, dear grandchild
On this special day,
That joy and love and laughter
Go with you on your way.

TUESDAY—JULY 23.

ON his first day at college, a young friend of ours, Grant, received a piece of advice from an experienced lecturer as he was told about the workload ahead:

"There's a lot to be done," he was told. "To get through it all, don't put your wishbone where your backbone ought to be."

Sound advice for life.

WEDNESDAY—JULY 24.

I OFTEN think it's good, during those times of trouble or stress, to have something amusing to take some of the strain and help us to laugh a little. Entertainers famous in the world of theatre and television certainly know the wisdom of that attitude. In the variety world comedy stars often relax by playing practical jokes on each other.

A story I like concerns the late Alec Finlay, a Scots comic, who had to use the dressing-room occupied during the week by fellow entertainer Jimmy Logan for a Sunday night concert at the Alhambra Theatre in Glasgow. Alec arrived to find that Jimmy had tied up all the drawers and wardrobes with thick rope, and had even put giant padlocks on all the cases.

But Alec got his revenge two nights later. He asked the orchestra to play "Happy Birthday" and sent Jimmy a dozen gift boxes, each packed with bits of the rope, and locked with the same padlocks.

What is life if we can't enjoy a bit of fun now and then!

THURSDAY—JULY 25.

THESE memorable quotations are worth thinking about today — and every day:

"To dream of the person we'd like to be is a waste of the person we are."

"Worry does not prevent disaster, it prevents joy."

FRIDAY—JULY 26.

IF you have a choice of two evils — choose neither. There has to be a better way.

SATURDAY—JULY 27.

I MUST confess that both The Lady of the House and I have great difficulty passing bookshops both new and second-hand without entering and exploring the treasure to be found on their shelves. And it was in a small second-hand bookshop one afternoon that we discovered the perfect present for a friend — a slim collection of poetry bound in green and lettered in gold.

Tucked inside was a hand-painted birthday card, on which was written in elegant copperplate script these lovely lines by the American poet Henry Longfellow from "The Arrow And The Song":

I breathed a song into the air,
It fell to earth, I know not where;
For who has sight so keen and strong
That it can follow the flight of song?

Long, long afterward, in an oak
I found the arrow, still unbroke;
And the song, from beginning to end,
I found again in the heart of a friend.

SUNDAY—JULY 28.

AFTER this manner therefore pray ye: Our Father, which art in heaven, Hallowed be thy name.

Matthew 6:9

COLOUR SUPPLEMENT

MONDAY—JULY 29.

ARE you making a journey today? A short journey, maybe, or you could be starting out on one that will take several hours. Here's some good advice, given to me by a friend who is a seasoned traveller:

"Always remember that the shortest way to travel anywhere is to have good company with you."

That way, the longest trips become so pleasurable you never count the hours!

TUESDAY—JULY 30.

ONE afternoon a minister was chatting to one of the elderly men standing near the local bridge. The topic of age came up and the man said: "I forget exactly how old I am, but I'm certainly an octo-geranium."

Later, the minister thought to himself — now, that means he's still growing, and he brings pleasure to those who meet him.

I can't think of a better description. Can you?

WEDNESDAY—JULY 31.

I WOULD like to share with you some wise words from the writer Katherine Mansfield:

"I am treating you as my friend by asking you to share my present minuses in the hope that I can ask you to share my future pluses."

Delightfully put, isn't it? The person who can cope with our shortcomings and problems surely deserves to share our good fortune, too.

August

THURSDAY—AUGUST 1.

I WATCHED a visitor in my garden one afternoon — a honey bee. It was quite oblivious to my nearness, so busy was it gathering the sweetness from the open blossoms. I thought of the hundreds of fellow busy bees gathering sweetness to turn into the delicious honey we all love.

Why can't mankind learn more from this industrious insect? Surely the world would be a much happier place if we could pay more attention to gathering the sweetness of life and spreading it.

Let's make a start today and gather and store the good, wholesome things in our hearts and minds.

FRIDAY—AUGUST 2.

EVERYBODY at the bus shelter that morning was complaining about the weather. Not surprisingly, perhaps, for it seemed to have been unseasonally dull and wet for weeks.

Only one old man was staying silent. At last, just as the bus was approaching, he said quietly, "So you would all prefer perpetual sunshine, would you? Well, look what it's done to the Sahara!"

SATURDAY—AUGUST 3.

A FRIEND likes to turn to heart-warming and inspiring quotations when he finds the going difficult or when he has been experiencing "a bad day". His favourite author is Victor Hugo, the French poet and novelist who wrote the classic "Les Miserables", and he finds these words particularly uplifting:

"Have courage for the great sorrows of life, and patience for the small ones. Then, when you have laboriously accomplished your daily task, go to sleep in peace, for God is always awake."

SUNDAY—AUGUST 4.

H IS name shall endure for ever: his name shall be continued as long as the sun; and men shall be blessed in him; all nations shall call him blessed.

Psalms 72:17

MONDAY—AUGUST 5.

T HE Lady of the House and I were once talking about a mutual acquaintance who travels a lot for pleasure, and I happened to say: "Yes, Bob must be sixty years old."

"You mean," replied the Lady of the House with a smile, "Bob is sixty years young." She then quoted the words of the American writer and essayist Oliver Wendell Holmes:

"To be seventy years young is sometimes far more cheerful and hopeful than to be forty years old."

TUESDAY—AUGUST 6.

MARTIN KEVILL has been described as a saint in a world of greed. He used to live in a caravan at the bottom of his garden in Lancashire, and then took up residence in a potting shed. After a lifetime's work, he gave the keys to his former home to a Catholic charity which has turned it into a home for the disabled.

"This is a selfish world," he said, "so I thought I would buck the trend and do something for someone else instead of myself."

Martin also created the Caring Millennium Dome. It comprises a holiday house, open all year round, free for children with learning difficulties and dedicated to the plight of the poor and disabled around the world. His Dome is flanked by the Ten Commandments on one side and the Sermon on the Mount on the other.

The spirit of the Caring Millennium Dome represents the wishes of so many in the early years of a new century.

WEDNESDAY—AUGUST 7.

THE Lady of the House and I went on an afternoon visit to a senior citizens' social club. We couldn't help but notice how happy everybody looked — some folk were chatting over coffee and cakes, while others were dancing. There was pleasant music in the background.

Later, as we left, we caught sight of this notice: "The trick is to make laughter outshine the tears."

That's a happy thought for everybody, whatever their age . . .

THURSDAY—AUGUST 8.

THAT silver tea-set was something Joan had never liked. It had been given to her as a wedding present many years before but, for one thing, the tea never seemed to taste as good as it should and, for another, it needed constant cleaning. Eventually, Joan put the tea-set up in the attic.

Her daughter, Emma, on the other hand, had always loved the silver tea-set and thought it most elegant. When she was married, Joan gladly gave the tea-set as a specially-requested wedding present. Thrilled, she immediately took it to a jeweller's to be valued for insurance purposes. It commanded quite a price.

So it would seem that the tea-set had three different values. For Joan it was worthless and she was glad to be rid of it. To the jeweller it was worth a substantial sum. But to Emma it was beyond price and she wouldn't have parted with it for a king's ransom.

Price and value are often two very different things.

FRIDAY—AUGUST 9.

THUMBING through a pile of old magazines one afternoon, I came across these wise words:

"Love isn't love until you give it away. Share some today."

Worthy words to keep in mind on any day of the year.

SATURDAY—AUGUST 10.

"THERE are so many expenses these days," sighed a neighbour, waving a couple of bills which had just been delivered.

However, the amazing thing is that there are still lots of things we can enjoy that cost nothing. For example, you don't have to pay each time you go to the park where there is beauty and fresh air. On the way you can admire window boxes, tubs and front gardens. Then again, you can spend satisfying time just chatting to a neighbour.

Now, try to think of more free delights to add to the list . . .

SUNDAY—AUGUST 11.

AND he took them up in his arms, put his hands upon them, and blessed them.
Mark 10:16

MONDAY—AUGUST 12.

IT was a beautiful morning, fresh and clear after early rain. The Lady of the House and I set off along the river bank, watching the swans glide across the water and listening to the birds. Sunlight sparkled on the water. I thought of some words I had come across by Chief Dan George:

"The beauty of the trees, the softness of the air, the fragrance of the grass, speaks to me. The faintness of the stars, the freshness of the morning, the dewdrop on the flower, speaks to me, and my heart soars."

May you have sunlit memories to cheer you, too, and may your hearts soar with the joy they bring.

TUESDAY—AUGUST 13.

"I DO dislike change!" our friend Iris stated. Exactly what we were discussing, I don't remember, but her words stayed with me.

I thought of them again when I came across this quotation. It comes from the late President Kennedy, who knew many changes in his short life: "Change is the law of life. And those who look only to the past or the present are certain to miss the future."

Wise words indeed. We would do well to remember them, and try to accept change graciously, to go forward cheerfully and hopefully!

WEDNESDAY—AUGUST 14.

ONE prisoner gave another a book of matches bearing the single word — *Courage!* The recipient had been very low, and that one small gesture of shared humanity was enough to restore hope. And when he was eventually released his defence lawyer, Peter Benenson, initiated an organisation built on a very simple principle.

Since its foundation in Britain in 1961, Amnesty International has offered hope. People in free countries can write letters to prisoners being held and even tortured for political reasons. For thousands of prisoners of conscience, the knowledge that someone cares — even an unknown letter-writer — is enough to kindle a flame of hope.

And all because someone passed on a message which said — *Courage!*

THURSDAY—AUGUST 15.

I CAME across this prayer one Sunday when I was leafing through some old church magazines and would like to pass it on to you today:

> *Lord, grant me I pray —*
>   *Courage when the best things fail me,*
> *Calm and poise when storms assail me,*
>   *Common sense when things perplex me,*
> *A sense of humour when they vex me,*
>   *Hope when disappointments damp me,*
> *Wider vision when life cramps me,*
>   *Kindness when folk need it badly,*
> *Readiness to help them gladly,*
>   *And when effort seems in vain —*
> *Wisdom to begin again.*

FRIDAY—AUGUST 16.

WHEN war broke out in 1914, there were many who were anxious to do something for their country. However, one French shepherd was considered too old to join the fighting forces. So what could he do instead, he wondered.

Every day as he looked after his sheep, he collected the acorns that lay around, and planted them in the scrubland where his flock grazed. During the years of conflict he planted thousands of trees — and today there are acres of forest to give testimony to his act of faith.

The old shepherd would never see the fruits of his labours. He just did what he felt was right — and what was within his powers to do.

SATURDAY—AUGUST 17.

A FAVOURITE piece of music worldwide is the Intermezzo from Cavalleria Rusticana, by the Italian composer Pietro Mascagni. Performed well, it is a tonic and a delight to hear.

An organ grinder began to play this famous piece one morning. And by accident — or by design? — he was standing below the window of the composer's flat. But he didn't play it well.

In fact, he played at such an unnaturally fast tempo that the composer dashed outside and turned the organ's handle at the correct speed. He told the organ grinder that, as he had composed the piece, he wanted it played correctly.

Next morning, the organ grinder was there again — right outside Mascagni's flat. This time he had a huge sign. It read: "Pupil Of The Celebrated Mascagni".

SUNDAY—AUGUST 18.

A ND the servant of the Lord must not strive; but be gentle unto all men, apt to teach, patient.

Timothy II 2: 24

MONDAY—AUGUST 19.

I REMEMBER with great pleasure our friend Margaret's description of the essence of friendship. "Friendship, Francis," she said, "is like a continuing conversation."

Don't these words say a lot about friendship — and also about Margaret?

TUESDAY—AUGUST 20.

ONE of our friends, Norman, is one of the most relaxed people you could ever come across. I asked him for the secret — why he seems to be on top of things and, at the same time, the sort of person who hasn't a single worry in the world.

Here was his answer: "The secret is to allow yourself enough time each day to be lazy and unproductive. Rest, for all of us, should be regarded not as a luxury but as a necessity."

Norman's advice is well worth taking. After all, isn't life for living, not scheduling?

WEDNESDAY—AUGUST 21.

A READER sent me this "Survival Kit", which a friend had commended to her:

A toothpick — to pick out good qualities in others.

A rubber band — it reminds us to be flexible.

First-aid dressings — to heal hurt feelings.

A pencil — reminds us to list our blessings every day.

An eraser — reminds us that we all make mistakes.

Mints — to remind us we are worth a mint to our loved ones.

A tea bag — reminds us to relax daily, giving us time to think about our blessings.

A survival kit which could surely see us through many a difficult time with some good advice for day-to-day life as well.

THURSDAY—AUGUST 22.

THE novelist Robert Louis Stevenson wrote many well-loved and enduring tales, among them "Treasure Island" and "Kidnapped". He also bequeathed us a number of interesting quotes about people and life in general. Among them is this little gem of wisdom:

"A happy man or woman is a better thing to find than a five-pound note. He or she is a radiating focus of goodwill; and their entrance into a room is as though another candle had been lighted."

Aren't we fortunate if we have encountered just such a person along the way?

FRIDAY—AUGUST 23.

NOWADAYS the Rev. Sabine Baring-Gould is remembered mainly as the author of the hymn "Onward Christian Soldiers". Yet in 1906 — some time before his actual death — he read an obituary stating that he had died at Port Elizabeth in South Africa. The death in question was really that of a cousin with a similar name, but the facts quoted in the obituary were certainly those of the clergyman's own life.

After reading the notice, he declared, "I find I have more friends than I knew of, so that the little error has softened my heart and made me thankful of a wider circle of such kindly feeling towards me than the little ring of my own family."

He would have been even more surprised to know that a society exists in his honour today both in London and Cornwall.

SATURDAY—AUGUST 24.

THESE words were inscribed on the front of the Viceroy's house in New Delhi:

In Thought *Faith*
In Word *Wisdom*
In Deed *Courage*
In Life *Service*

What better code could you find?

SUNDAY—AUGUST 25.

BUT the fruit of the spirit is love, joy, peace, longsuffering, gentleness, goodness, faith, meekness, temperance: against such there is no law.

Galatians 5:22-23

MONDAY—AUGUST 26.

THESE lines contain worthwhile sentiments for any day of the year, and I commend them to you today:

May you find time in each day to see beauty and love in the world around you;

May you realise that what you feel you lack in one regard, you may be compensated for in another;

May you learn to view everything as a worthwhile experience;

May you find enough inner strength to determine your own worth by yourself;

May what you feel you lack in the present become one of your strengths in the future.

Thoughts to keep in mind at any time.

TUESDAY—AUGUST 27.

HERE is something to think about, especially if you have been worrying about turning over that new leaf. The friend who passed it on to me says that it is well worth remembering, and I agree. It comes, I'm told, from an old Jewish proverb:

"Bad habits are easier to abandon if you tackle them today rather than tomorrow."

WEDNESDAY—AUGUST 28.

WHEN a Malaysian visitor first arrived in Britain she was struck by the beauty of the flowers growing on the banks as she approached Manchester during a long train journey. Coming from a country where flowers wilted all too quickly, she thought that she had rarely seen anything so fresh and beautiful. The flowers she so admired were, in fact, dandelions and daisies and she was horrified to learn we think of them as weeds!

I was reminded of Rudyard Kipling who wrote: "Give us delight in simple things", while Maria in "The Sound of Music" sang of some of her favourite things:

"Raindrops on roses and whiskers on kittens,
Bright copper kettles and warm woollen mittens,
Brown paper packages tied up with string . . ."

And to add one more apt quotation to this list, the prayer of poet George Herbert was:

"Thou who hast given so much to me, give one thing more, a grateful heart."

ROOTED IN THE PAST

THURSDAY—AUGUST 29.

IT is always a matter of interest to the Lady of the House and me when we come across a quotation where the author is "named" as being anonymous.

There must be thousands of such Mr, Mrs and Miss Anons in the world, and so often, the words they have written are well worth our attention.

Here's a little gem of anonymous wisdom, which we chanced upon one afternoon:

Life's battles don't always seem to go
To the strongest or fastest man,
But sooner or later the man who wins
Is the one who thinks he can.

FRIDAY—AUGUST 30.

ONE day, I came across this delightful thought and I'd like to share it with you: "a laugh is happiness set to music".

SATURDAY—AUGUST 31.

ONE FOR ALL

I HAVE an advisor,
A doctor, a friend,
Someone who will listen,
On whose help I depend.

A Father, companion,
Who always is there,
It's easy to reach Him,
For I just say a prayer.
                    Chrissy Greenslade.

September

THE Lord by wisdom hath founded the earth; by understanding hath he established the heavens.

Proverbs 3:19

"PHONE now, don't delay!", "Sale ends tomorrow!", "Hurry, hurry, hurry!" . . . Do you sometimes feel bombarded by all kinds of advertisements with this great sense of urgency — on television, radio and in the newspapers?

Are there days when you'd like to hold up your hands and say, "Slow down, please!"? I think the unknown writer of these words must have felt himself caught up in such a rush, and I sympathise:

"Slow me down, Lord, steady my hurried pace. Give me the calmness of the everlasting hills. Teach me the art of taking little vacations; of stopping to look at a flower; or taking time to chat to a friend or read a few lines from a good book. Inspire me to send my roots deep into the soil of life's enduring values, that I may grow towards the star of my greater destiny."

Just reading these sentiments makes me feel more peaceful, and I hope that you will feel the same.

MAKING A
SPLASH

TUESDAY—SEPTEMBER 3.

STAGE and screen comedians often throw in a wise word or two to add homely philosophy to their humorous patter. I once heard this from a performer on television who made it his final punchline:

"May you have the hindsight to know where you've been," he mused, "the foresight to know where you're going and, finally," — a dramatic pause here — "the insight to know when you've gone too far."

Good advice, indeed, and well worth the applause it received.

WEDNESDAY—SEPTEMBER 4.

WE are touched by angels,
Walk where angels tread,
They will guard and guide us
Through the days ahead.
In the times of sorrow,
As in the days of joy,
They bring hope and comfort
Nothing can destroy.
In the hours of darkness,
When our dreams have flown,
They bring peace and healing,
We are not alone.
Through the times of doubting,
Still they understand,
We are touched by angels,
Walking hand in hand.

Iris Hesselden.

THURSDAY—SEPTEMBER 5.

SIR Ernest Shackleton, who was a contemporary of Captain Scott, was an intrepid explorer of the wild and lonely regions of Antarctica in the early days of its exploration. Sadly, he died on his last voyage to that part of the world in 1922, and was buried in South Georgia, a little island just short of the Antarctic Circle. These are his inspiring words to consider and remember in our daily life:

"And for the future my passion to be successful and to give my best to whatever I turn my hand to is undiminished. Never for me the lowered banner, never the last endeavour."

FRIDAY—SEPTEMBER 6.

TIME is something we all pay heed to each and every day, so here are some wise thoughts on that subject which appeal to the Lady of the House and me:

Take time to think,
   It is the source of power;
Take time to play,
   It is the secret of perpetual youth;
Take time to read,
   It is the fountain of wisdom.
Take time to be friendly,
   It is the road to happiness.
Take time to laugh,
   It is the music of the soul;
Take time to give,
   It is too short a day to be selfish.

SATURDAY—SEPTEMBER 7.

WHILE enjoying a cup of tea with the Lady of the House and me, our friend Mary told us that she had just read an article about the Summer drought of 1995.

"It was remarkable, Francis," she said, "because farmers were disappointed with their crops, but archaeologists were pleased. You see, the unusual conditions showed up hundreds of ancient settlement sites which had been hidden for centuries. They had always been there, but we hadn't been able to see them."

Afterwards, I thought of Martyn Lewis, the newscaster, who wished that the news bulletins he read could all contain good news but, like the hidden ancient sites, the good things in the world were all too often passed by. We have to actively seek them out and bring them to the surface, rather as the drought did and, by discovering that they are there, it will be a better world for us to live in.

SUNDAY—SEPTEMBER 8.

BUT thou, O Lord, art a God full of compassion, and gracious, longsuffering, and plenteous in mercy and truth.

Psalms 86:15

MONDAY—SEPTEMBER 9.

DO not undermine your worth by comparing yourself with others. It is because we are different that each of us is special.

FIELD
DAY

TUESDAY—SEPTEMBER 10.

RODNEY has maintained his village shop for some 20 years. One day, he was asked how his business was doing.

"Well," he mused, "I haven't made enough to give it up, and I haven't lost enough to give it up, but I hope to do one or the other this year."

I am reminded of the man whose shop was destroyed in the great Chicago fire of 1871. He arrived at the ruins next morning carrying a table. He set it up amid the charred debris and put a big sign above it: "Everything lost except wife, child, and hope — business will resume as usual tomorrow morning."

Such optimism is to be greatly admired.

WEDNESDAY—SEPTEMBER 11.

HARVEST hymns are happy hymns —
With grateful hearts we say
Our special thanks for harvest time,
And all it means today.

The hard work and the waiting time,
The sowing of the seed,
And now the golden reaping time
That God has blessed indeed!

It shows if we have faith and trust,
And wait with patience, too,
We'll find our lives — like harvest time —
Will be enriched anew!

Elizabeth Gozney.

THE FRIENDSHIP BOOK

THURSDAY—SEPTEMBER 12.

HERE is an anonymous quotation which I came across one evening:

"A friend is someone who knows the song of your soul and sings it back to you when you've forgotten the words."

Doesn't that spell out, in exactly the right words, the kind of genuine friendship which we all love to treasure?

FRIDAY—SEPTEMBER 13.

I WAS making a house-warming visit to friends of ours one day — a bigger house had become necessary for Alistair and Norma's growing family, but it wasn't just the added space they were thrilled about. The house was on rising ground and faced west and, as the sun went down that evening, I was called to the window.

"There, look at that!" said Alistair. I caught sight of a glorious sunset, its glow reflecting off the banks of cloud stretching across the sky. "Isn't it marvellous?" he enthused. "I'd never fully realised how splendid a sunset can be, and do you know what I've discovered? You can't have a good sunset effect like that without a lot of cloud."

On my way home Alistair's words gave me a great deal to think about, for unwittingly he had spoken a great spiritual truth. Sunsets with their banks of cloud reflect life: think of those clouds of daily life as adding to the glory of the day's sunset, and then they won't seem nearly so grey and dispiriting.

THE FRIENDSHIP BOOK

SATURDAY—SEPTEMBER 14.

I LIKE the story of the car manufacturer Henry Ford, who one day paid a visit to Dublin in order to open a new orphanage. He gave $1000 towards the cost, but the local paper reported that he had given $10,000!

The paper apologised and asked if he'd like a correction to appear in the next edition. Not wishing to appear mean, Ford decided to give the extra $9000 to the orphanage with the proviso that this text should be engraved in the stone of the building:

"I was a stranger and you took me in."

SUNDAY—SEPTEMBER 15.

THE grace of the Lord Jesus Christ, and the love of God, and the communion of the Holy Ghost, be with you all. Amen.
Corinthians II 13:14

MONDAY—SEPTEMBER 16.

"ISN'T this weather something awful!" we often say. Certainly not many of us can avoid being influenced by the way we feel when we look outside and see the day's weather.

It may be bright and sunny in the morning, but by afternoon or even midday, it can all change to dark clouds and gloomy skies.

At such times I remind myself that people can nearly always beat the worst of any weather by creating a sense of sunshine indoors.

"The weather of your heart can determine the climate of your day."

TUESDAY—SEPTEMBER 17.

THE Roman Emperor Marcus Aurelius was a knowledgeable philosopher and a close observer of human feelings. Some of his advice for enjoying life have been preserved through the centuries and still applies to modern living. Here are two of his thoughts:

"Let not your mind run on what you lack as much as on what you have already."

"Adapt yourself to the things among which your lot has been cast and love sincerely the fellow beings with whom destiny has ordained that you shall share your life."

WEDNESDAY—SEPTEMBER 18.

I RECKON old Charles is one of the most enthusiastic gardeners I know. He's quite a philosopher, too. I was passing his garden one September day and paused to exchange a word with him as usual.

"There are yellow leaves on your cherry tree, Charles," I remarked. "Autumn colours are lovely, but it does mean Winter's on the way." I couldn't help adding that all too soon the tree's bare outline would be revealed.

"True," he replied, "and I'll tell you what — it reminds me of ourselves. As we get older, our finery is stripped away and the shape of our character is revealed. I'd better start thinking about my own character so that I won't mind it being visible when I reach the Winter of my life!"

OH, ROWAN
TREE

THURSDAY—SEPTEMBER 19.

NO-ONE could ever accuse the American President Franklin D. Roosevelt of not being a fighter. He battled against adversity most of his life, not only leading his country through the Great Depression and later the Second World War, but also waging his own personal struggle against the crippling after-effects of polio which had attacked him as a young man.

He always regarded physical aggression as a last resort. One story he was fond of recounting goes as follows: two Chinese men were arguing in the midst of a crowd. A stranger expressed surprise that no blows were being struck. "Ah, but you see," his friend replied, "the man who strikes first admits that his ideas have given out."

FRIDAY—SEPTEMBER 20.

JUST a single flake of snow, and soon the world around is transformed. Just a tiny drop of rain, but from those drops the rivers flow, and seas stretch from shore to shore.

Just one tiny step and a journey is begun. Just one hand held out in friendly greeting, and a chain of warmth is started. Just a single voice raised in protest at injustice can be joined by many more and achieve results to change the face of history . . .

So next time you are tempted to say, "Oh, my little efforts won't help", think again. Remember that delicate snowflake, so small, so fragile, yet full of such promise in its small beginning.

SATURDAY—SEPTEMBER 21.

TODAY, like any other, has come and it will pass as quickly as it has arrived. Each day moves on relentlessly to the next, which is why I would like to share with you now these wise words by the writer George William Childs:

"Do not keep the alabaster box of your love and friendship sealed up until your friends are dead. Fill their lives with sweetness. Speak approving, cheering words while their ears can hear them, and while their hearts can be thrilled and made happier. The kind things you mean to say when they are gone, say before they go."

SUNDAY—SEPTEMBER 22.

THIS is a faithful saying, and worthy of all acceptation, that Christ Jesus came into the world to save sinners; of whom I am chief.

Timothy 1 1:15

MONDAY—SEPTEMBER 23.

WHEN a new housing estate was being built, a larger space than usual was left between two of the houses. This soon became a dumping ground for general rubbish by the residents.

One day, someone was seen planting a few surplus bulbs. "Now, that's a good idea," said a neighbour, who promptly brought along a few bedding plants they didn't need. Others followed suit, and by the end of the season the rubbish tip had been transformed into a eye-catching garden.

Isn't it marvellous that what we might throw away can bring beauty into our lives?

TUESDAY—SEPTEMBER 24.

SOMETIMES, when I have not carried out a task to my own — or someone else's — complete satisfaction, I have excused myself by saying, "Well, I did my best."

Catherine Booth, granddaughter of William Booth, the world-famous founder of the Salvation Army, once told this thought-provoking story of a memorable early encounter with the formidable "General".

"How did you get on at the corps?" he asked. "Did you do anything?"

"Yes, Grandpa, I sang."

"How was it?" he asked.

"Well, I did my best," she replied.

"Did your best, Catherine? Anyone can do their best. You'll be no good if you can't do better than your best!"

A bit severe, perhaps, but he went on kindly, "You see, child, when you have God to help you, that's just what happens. Anyone can do their best, but if God is helping you, you can do better than your best."

With such a good example to follow, no wonder Catherine went on to achieve such great heights in "The Army".

WEDNESDAY—SEPTEMBER 25.

THIS thought is certainly worth keeping in mind:

"For every minute you are angry, you lose sixty seconds of happiness."

THURSDAY—SEPTEMBER 26.

A SCHOOLTEACHER friend asked her young pupils to practise their writing skills by composing an imaginary letter to their minister. Here are two that made her smile:

Dear Minister, — I liked your sermon on Sunday, especially when it was finished.

Robin, Age 11.

Dear Minister, — Please say in your sermon that Scott Paterson has been a good boy all week. I am Scott Paterson.

Scott, Age 9.

FRIDAY—SEPTEMBER 27.

CHANCE ENCOUNTER

My dear old friend, with what delight
Our comradeship has been renewed;
For many a time I've thought of you,
So wistfully, in pensive mood.
In ages gone, my trusted guide,
My mentor, you would take my hand,
To lead me down enchanted roads,
Into many an unknown land.
Then, with the passing years, alas,
Old friends, discarded, dropped away,
Along with all those roseate dreams
That never saw the light of day.
What bliss, then, in that dusty shop,
To find you . . . for in very truth,
You were the joy — beloved book —
And inspiration of my youth!

Kathleen O'Farrell.

SATURDAY—SEPTEMBER 28.

MARTIN is a friend who always says folk should stop wishing for the future and rather concentrate their thoughts on "today", "now", "the present". He once suggested memorising these words by Paul Ferrini from his book "Love Without Conditions":

"Happiness happens only in the present moment. If you are happy now, there is nothing else to accomplish. Indeed, if you become concerned about whether you will be happy tomorrow or even five minutes from now, you will forget to be happy now. All your scheming and dreaming takes you away from your present happiness."

SUNDAY—SEPTEMBER 29.

AND God made two great lights; the greater light to rule the day, and the lesser light to rule the night: he made the stars also.

Genesis 1:16

MONDAY—SEPTEMBER 30

OUR friend Moira is much in demand to join in when friends decide to hold a party. She makes everyone feel so much brighter when she is in their company.

But now Moira's happy secret is out — and it is all due to this verse seen on her kitchen wall . . .

Grant me a sense of humour, please,
The saving grace to see a joke,
To win some happiness from life,
And pass it on to other folk.

October

IN our church service we often sing "Dear Lord And Father Of Mankind", one of my favourite hymns. It must be liked by many other people, too, because it regularly features in the top ten of popular hymn surveys.

It was written by John Greenleaf Whittier, who lived in the United States in the 19th century. He was an active Quaker and humanitarian, who championed the anti-slavery cause. There's something about the words of "Dear Lord And Father Of Mankind" which seem to bring comfort, calm and reassurance to many situations and I particularly like this verse:

Drop Thy still dews of quietness,
Till all our strivings cease;
Take from our souls the strain and stress,
And let our ordered lives confess
The beauty of Thy peace.

May you experience peace of mind today.

LEND a hand to all your brothers,
Gladly cheer success in others;
Greet the sunshine — and the grey,
Moping never won the day.

Maurice Fleming.

THURSDAY—OCTOBER 3.

PERHAPS I would never have come across the old church that afternoon had it not been for the sight of the darkening sky. The first drops of rain and a distant peal of thunder had heralded a stormy spell, but safe sanctuary was suddenly in sight.

As I opened the door and walked in, a very sad sight met my eyes. The church was disused and deserted, the floorboards dangerously sloping and creaky while daylight shone through a hole in the roof where heavy rain came in.

For a while I sheltered as best as I could and I thought of all the events which had taken place there, the walls once resounding to hymn and prayer in this spiritual home of a once-thriving community. As the rain gradually petered out, a sunbeam entered, almost like a ray of celestial light, it seemed.

Even in its dilapidated state, this was still God's house and He would continue to be here, for He is everywhere, no matter how humble or unlikely the surroundings.

FRIDAY—OCTOBER 4.

TODAY may be shaping up well for you but perhaps it is not quite so bright for a friend or neighbour. I'm reminded of these words, by an unknown author:

"A smile is the light in your window that tells others there is a caring, sharing person inside."

The more lights we can have in our windows, the better.

SATURDAY—OCTOBER 5.

OUR friend Davina has a home under the flight path of wild geese, which appear at certain times of the year. She loves to watch the long skeins of birds, flying in formation, calling to each other in their strange and haunting way, and her heart seems to go with them.

Many of us, at some time or other in our lives, have surely longed to fly with the wild geese — high, free and away to escape the pressure of everyday living. We can't literally do that, of course, but we can switch off from daily stresses with the help of music, sport, gardening or handicrafts.

SUNDAY—OCTOBER 6.

LET not your heart be troubled: ye believe in God, believe also in me.

John 14: 1

MONDAY—OCTOBER 7.

WHEN the pace of life is getting you down isn't it a pleasure to hear a cheery voice? Here's a good way of putting it in the words of an old saying:

May you have warm words on a cold evening,
A full moon on a dark night,
And the road downhill all the way to your door.

Are you, I wonder, a sender of "warm words"? We should try to be and offer them in good measure, especially when someone with a problem finds that the going is nearly all "uphill".

TUESDAY—OCTOBER 8.

OUR friend Nell is one of the most contented people you could ever hope to meet. Whether at home with her family, or at work with colleagues in her busy office, she keeps pleasant and cheerful. It is a pleasure to know her.

I asked Nell to tell me her secret and explain exactly why she always looks so happy. She thought for a moment, then revealed the clever way she tackles each moment of every day.

"It's easy," she said. "I simply keep reminding myself that worry will never rob tomorrow of any sorrow it may bring, and that worry can also sap all our todays of their joy."

Now, isn't that a grand recipe for creating an attitude of happiness and contentment?

WEDNESDAY—OCTOBER 9.

MANY years ago a Methodist preacher gave me a book of essays entitled "Doorways To Happiness" by Peter Woods. They were first published in a popular weekly magazine. Some contain gems of wisdom that are still applicable years later — for example, two or three mention how "zest" adds to the quality of life.

This reminds me of a friend's remark about an orange cake she had made. "It's too bland," Dora decided after tasting the results. "I didn't put enough zest (orange peel) into the mixture."

Sometimes life's like that, isn't it? It can seem rather bland until we add more "flavour" by approaching things with a new enthusiasm.

THE FRIENDSHIP BOOK

THURSDAY—OCTOBER 10.

IT had been "one of those mornings" for Karen. They come to us all now and then, of course. The post brought a bill, much higher than anticipated. Then the front door lock jammed. Not least, poor Fluffie the cat was off colour — just not her usual self.

What a start to the day, Karen thought. Suddenly, a memory came to mind, that of a cross-stitched picture with words which her grandmother had hung on the wall for everyone to see. Its encouraging tone was as fresh as ever:

"Dark clouds gather and hide the sun, but beyond the clouds there is light — for everyone."

And you'll not be surprised to hear that Katie's bad start to the day was soon forgotten!

FRIDAY—OCTOBER 11.

OUR friend Jemima has been a nurse for most of her working life, and although she has been privileged to share many cheerful moments she has also been witness to times of sadness.

"When I first started my training," she once confided, "I was terribly worried that if anyone turned to me in distress, I wouldn't be able to cope — I wouldn't know what to say or do. It took me a little while to discover that most of the time I didn't actually have to say anything. I only had to be there."

What a valuable lesson to learn. Sometimes, simply taking the time to listen is far more important than "finding the right words".

PAWS FOR
THE CAMERA

SATURDAY—OCTOBER 12.

SIR DAVID FROST is well known for his interviews with the great and famous. He once said, however, that he did not really care who he interviewed since, as he put it, "Everybody has something to teach you if only you ask the right questions, be it a cab driver or a king."

SUNDAY—OCTOBER 13.

FOR ye know the grace of our Lord Jesus Christ, that, though he was rich, yet for your sakes he became poor, that ye through his poverty might be rich.

Corinthians II 8:9

MONDAY—OCTOBER 14.

THE PERSON WITHIN

*B*E *the person you want to be,*
  The person deep within,
Don't be afraid to face the world —
  Let the future begin!

Hitch your wagon to a star
  And follow where it leads,
Be strong of purpose, brave in heart,
  As every plan succeeds.

Time to be what you want to be,
  Step forward, take your cue,
The spotlight on, the curtain raised,
  The stage is set for you!

Iris Hesselden.

TUESDAY—OCTOBER 15.

THE Lady of the House was feeling rather under the weather one day. I offered a number of remedies and asked if I should call the doctor. However, she felt the best thing was to go to bed and take some extra rest.

"After all, Francis," she told me, "in my book of proverbs is this one — 'sleep is better than medicine'." So saying, she departed, clutching her hot-water bottle!

Not long after, I came across this proverb: "Sleep is a priceless treasure; the more one has of it, the better it is."

The following day I certainly had to agree with all these wise words. The Lady of the House was almost her usual cheerful self. I began to think that perhaps I might take a short nap myself. Just for medicinal purposes, you understand!

WEDNESDAY—OCTOBER 16.

SIR Lionel Luckham was the genial and much-respected High Commissioner for Guyana and Barbados, based in London. One day, he was listed as the principal speaker at a House Of Commons dinner during which the two speakers immediately before him had gone on at rather great length.

Finally, Sir Lionel stood up and announced to the diners: "My lords, ladies and gentlemen". Then he paused. "Your prayers have been answered."

And to deafening cheers he sat down again.

THURSDAY—OCTOBER 17.

GENEROUS is the spirit
That embraces all mankind.
Generous is the heart
When love is unconfined.
Generous with caring,
With forgiving, too,
Always understanding
And showing what to do,
Always having tolerance
Love takes a major role
Towards complete fulfilment,
When generous is the soul.

Jean Harris.

FRIDAY—OCTOBER 18.

"WE'LL gain an hour when we put the clocks back for Winter," is the usual conversation piece at this time of year. What better opportunity to reflect on the value of making the most of each and every hour of the day, whatever time of the year it may be.

Today, I'd like to share with you these words from the writer, H. Jackson Brown, who once scolded a young, time-wasting student into action when he retorted:

"Don't say you don't have enough time! You have, you know, exactly the same number of hours per day that were given to Helen Keller, Pasteur, Michelangelo, Mother Teresa, Leonardo da Vinci, Thomas Jefferson and Albert Einstein."

Well said, indeed.

SATURDAY—OCTOBER 19.

ONE morning, the vicar of a small country church climbed into the pulpit and looked at his congregation with a serious expression on his face. "Friends," he said, "it is with regret that I have to tell you of the death of one of our longest-serving church members, someone who was always recommended to do more than anyone else in the life of this parish. His departure will leave a gap in all our lives, a gap which we must all work to fill."

Then the vicar's face lit up with a smile. He said, "I am referring, of course, to our old friend Somebody Else. May he rest in peace. So I look forward to seeing you all for a short meeting after the service to plan this year's church fête."

The listeners understood the message, stayed for the meeting — and the fête turned out to be a huge success.

SUNDAY—OCTOBER 20.

FOR there is one God, and one mediator between God and men, the man Christ Jesus.
Timothy I 2:5

MONDAY—OCTOBER 21.

IT'S easy to feel that our own efforts are insignificant so remember these wise words:
"If you cannot do great things, do small things in a great way."
"Do what you can, where you are, with what you have."

TUESDAY—OCTOBER 22.

ISN'T it amazing what can be taught using computer graphics these days? A young friend had been given a computer programme in which the rudiments of riding skills were explained stage by stage. This was aimed at building up confidence as well as ability in the skill itself.

Only when familiarity and confidence had been well and truly implanted in the novice's mind was there mention of falling. A lesson on how to fall safely made the point that if you fall, you should remount at once.

Isn't that just like everyday life? We fall, many times, but in the words of the old song:

Pick yourself up
Dust yourself off
And start all over again.

WEDNESDAY—OCTOBER 23.

I OFTEN read nowadays about the population growing older and how large a proportion of senior citizens are to be found in our ranks. It is a result of better health all round — many of us can look forward to longer and healthier lives. But this does not mean leading a later life in idleness.

Ramon Blanco climbed Everest at the age of 62 and Louis Armstrong had a No. 1 hit song with "What A Wonderful World" when he was 66. Successful writer Mary Wesley published her first book when aged 70.

Maybe whe should coin a new phrase — "Life begins at 60!"

THURSDAY—OCTOBER 24.

A VISITING speaker at a social club once told her audience, "I'm no financial adviser, so I can't tell you how to double your money. But I can tell you how to double your troubles. It's easy — brood on them!"

The audience chuckled. They knew that this was often true. The speaker continued, "When troublesome thoughts fill your mind, try to think of something good or pleasant in your life, or something amusing. It won't always work, but this positive thinking can pay dividends — you could feel happier, even healthier. Now, what an investment that would be!"

FRIDAY—OCTOBER 25.

L ASALO BIRO was a Hungarian army officer. He and his colleagues were always hunting for a pen that would work in difficult situations — at high altitudes and under water. Being unable to find one, he enthusiastically decided to try to make one himself.

Lasalo had a brother, Georg, a chemist who eventually discovered a quick-drying ink that would rise or fall freely in the narrow tube that Lasalo had made — his ideal pen. This writing tool was only meant for military purposes, but it was immediately welcomed by the general public after the Second World War. Nowadays, most of us would not be without a ball-point pen!

Like Lasalo we should all keep on trying — not just with determination, but with enthusiasm.

SATURDAY—OCTOBER 26.

TREASURE CHEST

THINK of all the nicest things
That make a happy day.
A helping hand, a cheerful smile,
A greeting on the way.
The sunshine of the early morn,
The blossom on each tree —
Just add each joy, to make your day
A lasting memory . . .

Elizabeth Gozney.

SUNDAY—OCTOBER 27.

AND let the peace of God rule in your hearts, to the which also ye are called in one body; and be ye thankful.

Colossians 3:15

MONDAY—OCTOBER 28.

I WONDER if, like me, you enjoy all the gardening programmes on television and radio? As well as giving practical advice, I often find that there are many lessons for life to be learned.

For instance, it appears that sweetcorn, which is pollinated by the wind, does better growing in rows together rather than in a single row. Also, if broad beans are planted between two rows of peas, all close together, they support each other in strong winds.

How like life. Both in good times and difficult times, the closeness and support of family and friends are invaluable in helping us to stand firm.

TUESDAY—OCTOBER 29.

THERE are many sources for those in search of inspiring words, but one of the best must be the pages of church magazines. Here's one of the many examples I've found over the years:

No matter what misfortunes come,
What chores you have today,
What losses, trials, ills and spills,
May somehow come your way.
In spite of all you must deplore,
Let this be understood,
If you've the mind, you still will find,
There's always something good.

I found these soothing lines uplifting and hope that you will, too.

WEDNESDAY—OCTOBER 30.

SOME people are like a wheelbarrow — no use unless they are pushed. Others are like rugby balls — you just can't tell which way they will bounce next.

The most useful folk are like watches, quietly getting on with the job, always dependable, and full of good works!

THURSDAY—OCTOBER 31.

HERE, for today, is another gem from my scrapbook of memorable sayings:

"Hold fast all your dreams for, if your dreams ever die, life becomes a broken-winged bird that cannot fly."

November

A S Winter fast approaches I don't suppose many of us would regard it as their favourite time of year. But this season is not without its own joys, as Margaret Ingall's poem reminds us:

Dear Lord, please hear our song of praise
For all the crisp and Wintry days
For starry nights and sapphire dawns
For icicles and frosty morns,
For blue-tits bright and robins bold,
For brilliant skies of blue and gold
For glowing hearths and tabby cats,
For friends and fun and fireside chats,
For all these things we give you praise,
We thank you Lord, for Winter days.

I CAN'T tell you anything much about Marie, Marquise du Deffand, except that she was French, lived in the 18th century, and once said something that has encouraged many who have faced problems since.

Her advice was: "It is only the first step that is difficult."

Words that still have the power to inspire and spur us on today.

SUNDAY—NOVEMBER 3.

BUT he said, Yea rather, blessed are they that hear the word of God, and keep it.

Luke 11:28

MONDAY—NOVEMBER 4.

PHINEAS T. Barnum (1810-1891), the showman who ran "the greatest show on earth", put many clever ideas into his career as an impresario. He even bought 100 railway cars to take his circus performers and animals across the USA.

He surely outlined a golden rule for life when he said: "Whatever you do, do it with all your might. Work at it, early and late, in season and out of season, not leaving a stone unturned, and never deferring for one single hour that which can be done just as well right now."

TUESDAY—NOVEMBER 5.

THE long dark nights can be a cosy and a comfortable time with evening hours shared with family and friends, but it can also be a time of loneliness and sadness for many people.

Do you remember the hymn with the words: "You in your small corner and I in mine"? If we all were to make a few extra phone calls, write a few more letters or even send an e-mail or two, these rays of light might together touch other lives and kindle fresh hope in other hearts.

While we are happy and comfortable in our own homes, let us think of those less fortunate and do whatever we can to share our good fortune.

WEDNESDAY—NOVEMBER 6.

THE historian Thomas Babington Macaulay once remarked on a window at Lincoln Cathedral which was considered superior to every other window in the building. It is the Rose Window in the south transept, familiarly known as the "Bishop's Eye".

What is especially remarkable about it is that it consists of a medley of early stained-glass fragments, painstakingly fitted together some 200 years ago by an unknown apprentice, out of the pieces of glass which had been rejected by his master!

One person's rejects may often be just what another individual needs. Great things are so often made up of small fragments, fitted together like a giant jigsaw.

So many beautiful creations owe their origin to several sources which merge and knit together to become a part of what the poet John Keats called a thing of beauty and "a joy for ever".

THURSDAY—NOVEMBER 7.

OLD ALF has a very fine cherry tree in his garden. When I passed one day he was standing watching a number of blackbirds feasting on the ripe fruit.

"Don't you mind them eating up your crop?" I called.

"Not a bit," he replied. "Just think of the lovely songs they sing for me in return!"

A true nature lover.

LEST WE
FORGET

FRIDAY—NOVEMBER 8.

I LIKED this story in a Yorkshire magazine. A stallholder of mature years witnessed a near collision between two cars. He commented, "I reckon there were just as many reckless drivers when I was a lad — but they drove something that had more sense than they had. Horse sense!"

SATURDAY—NOVEMBER 9.

I ONCE heard a speaker describe each one of us as having a "light within". Sometimes, only a spark, but often something much brighter. She went on to tell us about her own son.

He is a talented musician, who studied at college and had before him a promising career. But after a trip abroad with a group of aid workers, he decided to take a different direction.

He now lives and works with sick and needy children in poor countries around the world. His musical skills, though, will never be wasted and he uses them whenever possible to help the young. He gave up his home, money and comfort to care for others and yet, as his mother told us, his light grows brighter each time she sees him.

May it continue to shine as a beacon of love.

SUNDAY—NOVEMBER 10.

O LORD, thou art my God; I will exalt thee, I will praise thy name; for thou hast done wonderful things, thy counsels of old are faithfulness and truth.

Isaiah 25:1

MONDAY—NOVEMBER 11.

LISTEN to the waves
  As they lap across the sand,
Listen to the wind
  As it gently cools the land.
Listen to the birds
  And all creatures of the earth,
Each one with a special voice
  That tells us of God's worth.
Listen to the young,
  Listen to the old,
Listen to the lonely
  And those out in the cold.
Listen to their message,
  Listen to their need,
Listen very carefully,
  Listen — and heed.

Jean Harris.

TUESDAY—NOVEMBER 12.

I AM a great admirer of Archbishop Desmond Tutu. His sermons are interesting and he has often used parables to get his message across. A favourite of mine concerns a member of a large orchestra who played the triangle.

He would wait while other instruments poured out their beautiful music then, at the conductor's request, he played his one note. "Ting!"

Nothing more, and yet an important part of the musical score. Doesn't this teach us that we all have a vital part to play in the great scheme of things, however small?

THE FRIENDSHIP BOOK

SIR Harry Lauder, the famous singer and comedian, often spoke timely words of advice to audiences during his world tours. When he visited the Rotary Club in Harrisburg, Pennsylvania, in 1916, he left his lunchtime audience with this thought:

"Go on in a way you are going. Leave your lights burning behind you, so that others coming after you may benefit thereby. Perchance, your boy or girl, passing that way some day, may point to a lamp you left and say, gratefully and with pride. 'My dad left that light burning'."

Now, aren't these wise words the kind which are really worth remembering?

A FRIEND keeps telling us that, next week or next month, she will be tackling a long-talked-about chore that is going to take most of the next twelve months to complete. However, we have been waiting for some time to see or hear that she has begun her self-appointed task.

In contrast, Catherine popped round one morning to push a little card of good wishes through the letterbox. It was just another of the many small gestures of help and friendship she brings to the lives of all who know her. She succeeds in doing — and completing — lots of small good deeds for friends and neighbours.

How true it is that the smallest deed is far greater than the grandest of intentions.

FRIDAY—NOVEMBER 15.

I SUPPOSE we all take things for granted sometimes. After all, we'd be more than a little surprised if the electric light didn't come on at the flick of a switch, for example.

Sometimes, though, taking things for granted can lead to disappointment or even hurt feelings — not receiving a birthday card we expected to get, or not being invited to a special party, perhaps.

When I catch myself taking things for granted or assuming the outcome of anything, I remember a former colleague. He had a motto in a frame hanging on his office wall. It read:

Never assume anything —
It may make an
ASS (of) U (and) ME.

SATURDAY—NOVEMBER 16.

OUR friend Liz went shopping, and found the two assistants serving behind the counter in apparently disconsolate mood.

Both looked quite forlorn, gave the impression that they were not enjoying their job and even the reluctant, "Good afternoon" which they managed to give her as she left, seemed somewhat forced.

Liz, however, was quite sympathetic and recalled this cheerful maxim given to her by her grandmother:

"When a person is too tired to give you a smile, give them one of yours. Nobody needs a smile so much as the person who has none to give."

SUNDAY—NOVEMBER 17.

I HAVE surely built thee an house to dwell in, a settled place for thee to abide in for ever.

Kings I 8:13

MONDAY—NOVEMBER 18.

TODAY I'd like to share with you these two quotations I came across in a magazine published a century and half ago:

"A soft answer breaks many a hard heart."

"Speak kind words and you will hear kind echoes."

TUESDAY—NOVEMBER 19.

A LITTLE while ago I received a letter from an American friend, Joe, telling how a car being driven by a mutual acquaintance had become stuck in snow after a heavy blizzard. All attempts to free it only resulted in the wheels getting more and more bogged down.

And then along came a young man who promptly set to work with a shovel, and got the car free again.

Joe reached for his wallet. "No way," the stranger said with a smile. "I belong to the Duo Club."

"Never heard of it," Joe remarked.

"Sure you have," came the reply. "It's the do-unto-others-as-you-would-have-them-do-unto-you club."

A lovely reminder of a golden rule for life.

WEDNESDAY—NOVEMBER 20.

A MAN in Wales was once given a tender shrub which had grown extremely well in a friend's garden. His friend had died, so in her memory he had accepted the lovely bush.

He cosseted it, with no immediate result, yet after three years it eventually produced a few buds. Unfortunately, a Spring frost occurred and damaged them. When Spring came around again, he covered the plant each night to give protection from the frost and, sure enough, after all that time he was rewarded with some beautiful blooms.

He said to me, "Francis, in spite of the soil and the weather, there is one thing that takes root in all gardens — and that is hope." It can grow in every heart, too, if we only keep on trying when at first we don't succeed.

THURSDAY—NOVEMBER 21.

WE don't always achieve all our dreams when we're young — sometimes we only "catch up" when we're older. This was certainly the case with my old friend Jack who had always wished he could play the piano, but the opportunity to learn had never been there at the right time.

In retirement he told me that things were different; he'd bought himself an old second-hand piano and was taking lessons. They would probably have been a bit of a struggle in his younger, busier days, but now they gave him a positive focus and he was looking forward to being able to play the odd tune or two.

FRIDAY—NOVEMBER 22.

I ENJOYED a fascinating book about traditional English customs. One custom which was new to me described the annual service for clowns, held in London. It certainly captures the imagination.

Sometimes, as many as 50 clowns — amateur and professional, in full costume and make-up — attend. They sing hymns and read the lessons. At the end of the service one year came the following prayer, shared by them all:

"Dear Lord, I thank You for calling me to share with others Your most precious gift of laughter. May I never forget that it is Your gift and my privilege."

They are right about how important laughter is in our lives. Whether we share it with clowns in baggy trousers or comedians in smart suits, or simply with our own friends, it is precious.

SATURDAY—NOVEMBER 23.

BUILDING WORK

FRIENDSHIP'S rather like a house,
  It needs a solid base
On which participants can put
  Sincerity in place.
But once cementing has been done
  And people work together,
It's bound to stand the test of time
  In any kind of weather.

J.M. Robertson.

SUNDAY—NOVEMBER 24.

AND without controversy great is the mystery of godliness: God was manifest in the flesh, justified in the Spirit, seen of angels, preached unto the Gentiles, believed on in the world, received up into glory.

Timothy 1 3:16

MONDAY—NOVEMBER 25.

IT was an old seafaring man I heard give this piece of good advice. Helpers were needed for a project and somebody had said, "Just leave me out. I couldn't do much."

It was then Ben said, "Every hand counts. Remember, a small tug can bring a huge liner into harbour."

TUESDAY—NOVEMBER 26.

ONE of the best known and most successful drama critics of the 20th century was James Agate. One day, a young man asked him how to become a successful dramatic critic.

James Agate replied that he must study the works of at least thirty great dramatists to discover what great drama is, and only then could he dare to become a critic at all.

"But I'll be at least forty before I get through such a list!" the young man objected. Agate then replied, "You must be at least forty before your opinions have any value."

What an astute reply – there is no easy way to success in life, in whatever field. Hard work and experience are best.

TOUCH OF
FROST

WEDNESDAY—NOVEMBER 27.

NO day for me is complete without a little quiet reading, before I switch off the lights, and go upstairs. I wonder if you know these words from the Victorian cleric and writer, Charles Kingsley? I came across them one November evening:

"A blessed thing it is for any man or woman to have a friend, one whom we can trust utterly, who knows the best and worst of us, and who loves us just the same."

Such a friend, I think you'll agree, is to be valued far above gold and diamonds.

THURSDAY—NOVEMBER 28.

SOME reasons to be cheerful
On a dreary Winter's day:
The first hot tea or coffee
To chase the blues away.
Perhaps a letter in the post,
That would be a surprise!
Or meeting someone pleased to see you,
Welcome in their eyes.
Something hot and tasty
And tempting for your tea,
A quiet evening by the fire,
A chocolate — or three!
The prospect of a restful sleep,
A warm and cosy bed,
A brighter day tomorrow,
And better times ahead.
Iris Hesselden.

FRIDAY—NOVEMBER 29

ROBERT Milligan, a Mayor in New Zealand, was visiting London one day when his attention was caught by the statue of Peter Pan in Kensington Gardens. It occurred to him that something like it would not be amiss in his home city, so made a few enquiries.

Sir James Barrie, the author of Peter Pan, saw no problems and a London sculptor was engaged to fashion a bronze statue called Wonderland. But who should he use for his models?

The sculptor thought of Sam, his newspaper boy. Sam had a younger sister, Alice, who would often play nearby. For over 70 years the features of Alice and her brother Sam have adorned the Wonderland statue in the public gardens of Oamaru on the South Island of New Zealand.

No-one is ever too old to wonder!

SATURDAY—NOVEMBER 30.

A PLEASANT greeting and a willingness to listen — these are attributes to cultivate. Freda is almost housebound, but she never allows restrictions to rule her life and has many friends who call seeking her advice. One day I asked her where she got her love of life from.

"Do you really need to ask?" she replied quietly. "Every morning when I get up I say this same little prayer — 'Lord, bring me today someone I can help,' and He does."

People like Freda are the best helpers of all — they have time to listen to others.

December

SUNDAY—DECEMBER 1.

BLESSED are the peacemakers: for they shall be called the children of God.

Matthew 5:9

MONDAY—DECEMBER 2.

DURING the Second World War, Jennifer Stanley was a child who was a patient in a little cottage hospital in Lincolnshire.

On the wall opposite her bed, someone with an offbeat sense of humour had hung Jennifer's gas mask. She was very ill; she wouldn't eat; and she didn't seem to be interested in anything, until one morning a little dove flew through the window and landed on the gas mask. Then it popped inside. Later, the dove flew out of the window again and vanished.

Every morning for three weeks the dove returned to the gas mask, and Jennifer, with something to hold her attention, began to perk up. Three dove's eggs were found inside that gas mask a couple of weeks later.

That dove had unwittingly used the ugly symbol of war as a cradle for new life — and in the process had helped a little girl back to health and happiness.

TUESDAY—DECEMBER 3.

THIS memorable quotation is from a speech by the great motor-car manufacturer Henry Ford: "My best friend is the one who brings out the best in me."

WEDNESDAY—DECEMBER 4.

CHARLOTTE MARY was nineteen years old when she married William, a young naval officer, who served under Nelson. Their marriage was a true love match, yet much of it was spent apart, when William was at sea.

On the birth of their first child, William gave Charlotte a gold posy ring engraved with their entwined names, and set with six small precious stones — a ruby, an emerald, a garnet, an amethyst, another ruby, and a diamond. The first letters together spell "regard", a word implying love and respect.

William and Charlotte's marriage was long and happy. They would have agreed with these words written by Martin Luther: "There is no more lovely, friendly, and charming relationship, communion, or company, than a good marriage."

Now, perhaps you are wondering how the Lady of the House and I came to know about Charlotte and William. Well, they were the great-grand-parents of Great-Aunt Louisa, whose scrapbooks we cherish. Charlotte's posy ring is now the much-loved possession of a modern-day Charlotte, who is happily married to Bill who serves in the Navy!

THURSDAY—DECEMBER 5.

"SOMETIMES I sits and thinks and sometimes I just sits," says a wise saying. The inner mind is surely marvellous. While we quietly sit back, it is ticking away. Consider for a moment some of the achievements which have resulted from people being quiet and simply thinking.

Seeking peace for his troubled soul, Galileo sat quietly all those centuries ago, and the gentle rhythmic movement of a swinging lamp nearby gave him the idea of a pendulum swinging to and fro as a means of measuring the passage of time.

Isaac Newton was quietly resting when he saw an apple fall and thus began to grasp the idea behind his law of gravity. James Watt was relaxing in his kitchen when he saw steam lifting the top of a kettle and thus the idea of power to drive a steam engine was born.

So don't feel guilty next time you want to "just sit quietly". Many problems are solved, new ideas come to mind, and vitality is often revived by doing exactly that!

FRIDAY—DECEMBER 6.

SENECA wrote: "A poor man is not one who has little but one who longs to have too much. Always remember that money has never yet made anyone rich.

"Let each day be lived as though it were the last in a long line of a happy fulfilling life. If God grants us another tomorrow let us remember to accept it with a happy heart."

SATURDAY—DECEMBER 7.

A MINISTER I know likes to welcome children to morning service on Sundays. He realises it may be difficult for them to pay attention for long, so quite naturally he sends them off to Sunday school after the second hymn. For this a children's hymn is chosen.

One Sunday morning there happened to be no children present, so the minister decided on a last-minute substitution. He solemnly announced, "As there are no children present, instead of the hymn chosen for them we will sing 'Now Thank We All Our God!'" It raised a smile but our minister friend always gives thanks when there are plenty of children present at other times.

SUNDAY—DECEMBER 8.

A FOOL uttereth all his mind: but a wise man keepeth it in till afterwards.

Proverbs 29:11

MONDAY—DECEMBER 9.

IT'S Winter time, it's the final month of the year, and all round the world people are getting into the spirit of the festive season.

As we prepare to join friends and family amid the colourful decorations, well-laden tables, crackers and mistletoe, I think it is the right time to remind ourselves of these wise words by an unknown writer:

"He who has not Christmas in his heart will never find it under a tree."

A thought for all of us in December.

WEB OF
WONDER

TUESDAY—DECEMBER 10.

THIS is my road,
  Where will it wind?
When I come to a turning
  What will I find?
Will there be shadows?
  Will it be bright?
Will forests or mountains
  Filter the light?
I look forward with pleasure
  For this much I know,
He will be with me
  Wherever I go.

                    Jean Harris.

WEDNESDAY—DECEMBER 11.

IN the festive season, isn't it a pleasure to take a leisurely walk past the Christmas lights and spend time just looking at the windows of the big stores. That's when you often get an inkling of the less serious-minded spirit that is all around at this time of year, too.

One December afternoon the Lady of the House and I smiled as we caught sight of a sign outside a toy store: *"Ho, ho, ho spoken here!"*

We had to smile as those five simple words made us actually almost hear the infectious chuckle of Santa's voice. The Lady of the House and I were transported back again to our own childhood, completely content with the world and everything around us. That, surely, is the best of moods as Christmas approaches.

THURSDAY—DECEMBER 12.

ONE cold day, the Lady of the House and I called to see our young friend Vicky who was busily tidying her bookshelves. Some volumes she put aside for a charity shop, but her treasured items she dusted and carefully put back.

A small book caught my eye. It contained verses by A. A. Milne with the delightful drawings of Winnie The Pooh. I opened it at the following:

"Oh, the butterflies are flying, now the Winter days are dying and the primroses are trying to be seen," and a little further on there was: "Oh, the honeybees are humming on their little wings and humming that the Summer, which is coming, will be fun."

I asked Vicky if she would be giving this away.

"Certainly not," she replied. "If I'm feeling a little down, Winnie The Pooh always cheers me up." As I struggled against the wind on the way home, I knew what she meant as I recited to myself: "And the Summer which is coming will be fun."

Thank you, A. A. Milne — or do I mean Winnie The Pooh? They seem to be inseparable.

FRIDAY—DECEMBER 13.

OUR friend Beth's three-year-old daughter needed entertainment. "Go and give the gardener a hand," suggested my friend. Minutes later, she found a distressed young girl crying, "I don't want to give Ned a hand — I need them myself!"

SATURDAY—DECEMBER 14.

ONE cold December night in 1914, a fire broke out in Thomas Edison's factory – soon everything was destroyed.

Next day Thomas spoke to all his employees: "We're going to rebuild! We'll make capital out of this disaster — the rubbish will be cleared out and then we'll build a bigger and better factory on the ruins." He then rolled up his coat for a pillow and fell asleep on a table.

What an example us all! Thomas Edison was a man who absolutely refused to be defeated. We, too, must try not to be discouraged by setbacks.

SUNDAY—DECEMBER 15.

NOW therefore ye are no more strangers and foreigners, but fellow citizens with the saints, and of the household of God.

Ephesians 2:19

MONDAY—DECEMBER 16.

I LIKE the story Peter Ustinov told about a performance of his in New Zealand. He had just started when there was a power cut.

Peter calmed the audience by telling them to imagine a sleepless night. They had switched off the light and turned on the radio to hear him.

He got more laughs than when he could be seen and added that he regretted that the lights did not fail more often! What an effective way of showing the power of words, especially when spoken by a powerful voice.

TUESDAY—DECEMBER 17.

A CLASS of six-year-olds was preparing a scene for a Nativity play one Christmas. To get them thinking, their teacher asked them to draw some ideas of what the scene should represent.

One enterprising lad drew Joseph as a carpenter surrounded by lots of tools, including an electric drill. His teacher, on examining the picture, exclaimed, "It's a good picture, Mike, but there was no electricity in those days!"

Mike promptly explained, "But this is a cordless one!"

WEDNESDAY—DECEMBER 18.

I T was raining when the Lady of the House and I called in one afternoon to see our friend Laura, and found her addressing a mountain of envelopes to go with an enormous pile of Christmas cards.

I complimented her on her efficiency and she laughed. "Ah, but Francis, it's not a chore — it's a pleasure," she explained.

"After all, what could possibly be a nicer way to spend a wet December day than sitting by the fireside remembering happy times with friends and family? And it's even better when I receive cards and letters back sharing news and memories."

As the Lady of the House later remarked, it's certainly a far more effective way of bringing a sparkle to Christmas than simply hanging up tinsel!

SPLENDOUR

THURSDAY—DECEMBER 19.

AS the year draws to a close, many of us will be thinking of choosing a new diary. Henry Wansborough, writing for the Bible Reading Fellowship, offers this advice:

"It is most important for the Christian life, to be sure that the calendar or diary you buy begins the week on a Sunday, not a Monday. Sunday is not just the tail end of the week, to be spent recovering from Saturday night and gearing up for the toil of Monday. It is not even a day of rest: the Jewish Sabbath, when God rested from his labour of creating, was Saturday. For the Christian, the week begins on Sunday, because then is the celebration of the Lord's resurrection, the beginning of new life."

FRIDAY—DECEMBER 20.

OUR friend Henry's beautiful hand-painted Christmas card contained the old saying:

"So many mince pies as you taste at Christmas, so many happy months you will have."

I smiled again when I read Henry's postscript. "Grace and I have all the grandchildren staying with us for Christmas, and I am just discovering the truth of the words — 'I am not young enough to know everything'!"

By the way, the Lady of the House and I think that we will be able to eat, without too much difficulty, twelve mince pies over the Twelve Days of Christmas, to give us twelve happy months in the coming year!

THE FRIENDSHIP BOOK

A S Christmas approached one year, a parish council decided that they would illuminate their village and all the residents were asked to donate the cost of one light. If everyone contributed the high street could be lit up.

People were happy to give a small amount and were pleased with the result — coloured lights casting a glow on their cottages, church and shops. The minister took co-operation as the theme for his sermon, explaining that one or two lights would have little impact, but when everyone contributed a little the effect was magnificent.

It is true that individually one can do just a little to light up the world, but when united we can fully illuminate even the darkest places.

B EHOLD, a virgin shall be with child, and shall bring forth a son; and they shall call his name Emmanuel, which being interpreted is, God with us.

Matthew 1:23

T HE Star of Bethlehem rose high
  As shepherds' homage drew them nigh
 To see the babe in lowly stall,
And hear the angels' voices call
 A benediction for the birth
Of little Jesus, King on earth.

Elizabeth Gozney.

TUESDAY—DECEMBER 24.

CHRISTMAS cards are always a pleasure to receive and bring a ray of light into dark December days. One year a card arrived from the north-east of England, a part of the country where snow tends to come early!

This is the message which appealed to us: "May the true meaning of Christmas bring a new warmth to your world and to the world of those you love." Only a few words, but don't they sum up all those things we try to say to each other?

I would like to pass them on to you with an added wish for your happiness in the coming year.

WEDNESDAY—DECEMBER 25.

CHRISTMAS thoughts are flowing
Out to those we love,
Christmas magic growing,
Bright stars shine above.
Memories of other times
Many songs were sung,
Candlelight and silver chimes —
When the world was young.

Wishing joy and love and peace,
Happiness to share,
Hoping blessings all increase,
Goodwill everywhere.
Christmas love is flowing
Touching heart and hand,
May it keep on growing —
Filling every land.

Iris Hesselden.

TOMORROW
IS ANOTHER
DAY

THURSDAY—DECEMBER 26.

GROWING older has its compensations and in the same way there surely comes a sense of wonder when each day grows old and each month moves on, towards the end of the year. Here are two sayings to ponder:

"It is when each day is old and far spent that it displays the golden colours of sunset."

"It is when the year is old and has run its course that Mother Nature transforms the world into a fairyland of snow."

FRIDAY—DECEMBER 27.

THERE is a place for dreams, but as an old proverb says: "To believe only one's dreams is to spend all of one's life asleep."

There is a time for dreaming — and a time for doing.

SATURDAY—DECEMBER 28.

THE American clergyman and writer, Rev. Edward Everett Hale, established the "Lend-A-Hand" charity movement with its motto: "To look up and not down, to look forward and not back, to look out and not in, and to lend a hand."

In the words of another maxim from this writer:
"I am only one, but still I am one.
I cannot do everything,
But still I can do something;
And because I cannot do everything,
I will not refuse to do the something
    that I can do."

SUNDAY—DECEMBER 29.

IN every thing give thanks: for this is the will of God in Christ Jesus concerning you.

Thessalonians I 5:18

MONDAY—DECEMBER 30.

BEGIN AGAIN

LET us cast aside the hurts
  That rankle in the heart.
Let's try to mend old quarrels
  And make another start.
Forgiving the old grudges
  And bitter words once said,
Decide to fill our life with love
  And happiness instead.

Harbouring resentment will
  Destroy our peace of mind,
We find our views distorted
  Unloving and unkind.
Forgiveness is the gentle balm
  That comes like fresh Spring rain,
Blessing all within its reach
  When we begin again.

Kathleen Gillum.

TUESDAY—DECEMBER 31.

AS the year draws to a close, The Lady of the House and I hope that your world in the coming year will be poor in loneliness, and rich in caring, compassion, charity, courage, hope, love and peace. We both wish you health and happiness, friendship and love.

The Photographs

MAKING TRACKS — *Holme Chapel, Lancashire.*
MIST AND MOUNTAIN — *Loch Shiel, near Glenfinnan.*
NOT A CLOUD IN SIGHT — *Malham Cove, Yorkshire.*
MELLOW YELLOW — *View from Middlesmoor, Down Nidderdale.*
UP THE GARDEN PATH — *Near Eastnor, Herefordshire.*
FLORAL TRADITION — *A Well Dressing Plaque,*
Ashford In The Water, Derbyshire.
CLIMB EVERY MOUNTAIN — *Sgurr Ban and Mullach Coire Mhic*
Fhearchair, Ross and Cromarty.
WANDERING FREE — *Watendlath, Cumbria.*
REST A WHILE — *Loch Lomond.*
RAMBLER'S HEAVEN — *Wensleydale, Yorkshire.*
FLOWER POWER — *Luss, Dunbartonshire.*
COLOUR SUPPLEMENT — *Perth.*
NATURE'S TAPESTRY — *Pitmedden Gardens, Aberdeenshire.*
ROOTED IN THE PAST — *Crathes Castle and Gardens, near Banchory.*
FIELD DAY — *Gillamoor, North Yorkshire.*
OH, ROWAN TREE — *Glen Coe.*
LEST WE FORGET — *Commando Memorial, Spean Bridge.*
TOMORROW IS ANOTHER DAY — *Bradda Head, Isle Of Man.*

ACKNOWLEDGEMENTS: **Alvey & Towers Picture Library;** Paws For The Camera. **Aurora Travel Photography;** Lunch Break. **Terence J. Burchell;** Promise Of Spring. **Jacqui Cordingley;** Making Tracks. **E. W. Charleton;** Tomorrow Is Another Day. **Carol Claffey;** Still Life; Making A Splash. **Chris Cole;** In The Driving Seat. **J. T. Davey;** Old Rugged Cross. **Paul Felix;** Up The Garden Path. **V. K. Guy;** Wandering Free. **T. G. Hopewell;** Rest Awhile, Flower Power. **C. R. Kilvington;** Not A Cloud In Sight, Mellow Yellow, Rambler's Heaven, Field Day, Oh, Rowan Tree. **Douglas Laidlaw;** Mist And Mountain. **Malcolm Nash;** Flying Colours, Climb Every Mountain, Colour Supplement. **Oakleaf Photography;** Nature's Tapestry, Rooted In The Past. **Polly Pullar:** Splendour. **F. Smith;** Touch Of Frost. **Sheila Taylor;** Lest We Forget, Animal Magic. **Richard Watson;** Web Of Wonder. **Andy Williams;** Floral Tradition.

Printed and Published by D. C. Thomson & Co., Ltd.,
185 Fleet Street, London EC4A 2HS.
ISBN 0-85116-783-7